Human resource strategies for international growth

Internationalization is often seen as posing distinctive human resource problems that are difficult to overcome. In contrast, this book is written in the belief that there are many basic similarities and continuities between domestic and international business, and that identifying these reveals generic processes and skills which are the basis for escaping from the domestic setting.

Unlike much existing literature, *Human resource strategies for international growth* considers the problems of internationalization as they affect large and small firms, newly internationalizing firms and those which are mature in the international arena. The implications of the Single European Market are explored and relevant theories are explained to reveal the what, why and how of internationalization.

Drawing on original research and an extensive review of the literature, this book offers a comprehensive and critical overview of human resource issues in internationalization which will appeal to business students from first degree level to MBA.

Chris Hendry is associate director and principal research fellow at Warwick Business School, University of Warwick. He has co-authored a number of major reports including *Human Resource Development in the Small-to-Medium Size Enterprise* (1991).

The Routledge series in analytical management
Series editor: David C. Wilson
University of Warwick

This series is a welcome new resource for advanced undergraduate and post-experience students of management who have lost patience with 'off the shelf' recipes for the complex problems of strategic change. Individual series titles cross-reference with each other in a thoroughly integrated approach to the key ideas and debates in modern management. The series will be essential reading for all those involved with studying and managing the individual, corporate and strategic problems of management change.

Other titles available in the series

A Strategy of Change
Concepts and controversies in the management of change
David C. Wilson

What is Strategy and Does it Matter?
Richard Whittington

Technology and Organization
Power, meaning and design
Harry Scarbrough and F. Martin Corbett

Strategies of Growth
Maturity, Recovery and Internationalization
Peter McKiernan

Forthcoming

Competitiveness and Chaos
Walter Dean and Richard Whipp

Managing Culture
David Cray and Geoffrey Mallory

Human resource strategies for international growth

Chris Hendry

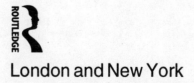

London and New York

First published 1994
by Routledge
11 New Fetter Lane, London EC4P 4EE

Simultaneously published in the USA and Canada
by Routledge
29 West 35th Street, New York, NY 10001

© 1994 Chris Hendry

Typeset in Baskerville
by LaserScript Limited, Mitcham, Surrey
Printed and bound in Great Britain by
Mackays of Chatham PLC, Chatham, Kent

British Library Cataloguing in Publication Data

A catalogue record for this book is available from the British Library.

ISBN 0-415-09773-8   ISBN 0-415-09774-6 (Pbk)

Library of Congress Cataloging in Publication Data

Hendry, Chris
  Human resource strategies for international growth / Chris Hendry.
    p. cm. – (Routledge series in analytical management)
  Includes bibliographical references and index.
  ISBN 0-415-09773-8   ISBN 0-415-09774-6 (Pbk)
  1. International business enterprises–Personnel management.
I. Title. II. Series
HF5549.5.E45H46   1994
658.3–dc20   93-17072
                                                        CIP

Contents

Figures

Tables

Acknowledgements

The author and publishers would like to thank the following for the use of material in this book:

Michael Pietsch of Warwick Business School for permission to reproduce Figures 3.1 and 3.2; John Wiley & Sons for permission to reproduce Table 3.1 from V. Pucik (1988) 'Strategic Alliances, Organisational Learning, and Competitive Advantage: The HRM Agenda', *Human Resource Management* 27 (1): 77–93; Kevin Barham and David Oates for permission to reproduce Table 4.3, 'Preparing managers for international postings', from The Ashridge Survey 1989–90; the publishers of *International Management* for permission to reproduce Tables 5.3, 6.2. and 6.3 from T. Lloyd, A. Carton-Kelly, and M. Mueller (1991) 'EC Heavyweights' (April): 26–67.

The author would also like to thank the Department of Employment for funding the literature review on which sections of this book are based.

Introduction

Internationalization is often seen as posing distinctive issues for a firm that are troublesome to surmount. The treatment of internationalization from a human resources point of view thus dwells on such problems as the selection, training, and management of expatriates; managing organizational complexity in the multinational; and managing joint ventures and other forms of strategic alliance.

The assumption that managing the international business, as opposed to the domestic, is different and more difficult blinds us to many basic similarities and continuities between domestic and international business. If we take as our focus the processes by which firms internationalize and sustain their international operations, we get a different perspective than if we focus on the specific tasks of the human resources function. This perspective exposes fundamental regularities between domestic and international business.

Identifying these regularities is important for international growth for the following reasons:

- it reveals generic processes and skills which are the basis for escaping from the domestic setting;
- it suggests how the domestic environment and analogous settings can be used to develop these skills; and
- it identifies organizational weaknesses which stand in the way of such development.

If these commonalities, opportunities, and blocks are recognized, it can help firms to think more positively about becoming international and to address relevant skills through their present systems for developing managers. Equally, it can help those in the educational and training business, in the universities and business schools, to develop activities, tasks, and situations for international management education.

A principal aim of this book is therefore to trace the similarities and regularities that exist between domestic and international business, and to follow through the implications for human resource management (HRM). These similarities/regularities can be described in terms of the different contexts in which internationalization manifests itself. Identifying these different contexts, moreover, highlights basic similarities and generic skills between different levels of internationalization. The book identifies six such 'contexts':

1 the leveraging of domestic competitive advantages;
2 initiating and sustaining international commitment;
3 networking in the newly internationalizing firm;
4 networking and learning in alliances and international joint ventures;
5 managing complexity in the international firm;
6 developing inter-cultural competence.

Each of these contexts defines particular issues for HRM. After Chapter 1, which provides an overview, Chapters 2–4 develop these contexts and issues according to a sequence which reflects the development of firms from being purely domestic to becoming progressively more internationalized. Chapter 2 considers how firms take the first steps towards internationalization. It thus embraces contexts 1, 2 and 3 above – the idea of internationalization as the leveraging of domestic competitive advantages, initiating international commitment, and the role of networking in developing international business. Chapter 3 takes this forward by looking at processes of networking and learning in alliances and international joint ventures, with the different issues for small and large firms arising from the way they use alliances. Chapter 4 then looks at the issues for the truly international firm in terms of the last two 'contexts' – managing complexity, and developing inter-cultural competence among staff.

The treatment of these 'contexts' not only reveals continuities and similarities for HRM between the international and domestic business environment, it identifies certain recurrent themes across the different levels of internationalization. Internationalization at all levels involves similar processes and the need for certain generic skills. These centre on networking, the role of teams, and organizational learning.

Large international firms, for instance, need to be able to mobilize, within their internal structures, knowledge accumulated in a variety of networks, and apply these both to new markets and to gain better synergies in existing ones. Newly internationalizing firms need to practise networking skills externally to build up the knowledge of customers and suppliers on which new business depends. Firms in alliances need to be able to access knowledge and transfer it through a network of personal exchange relationships. All of these processes involve networks, geared to learning, in which teams facilitate the conversion of information from individual sources into 'organizational' learning. Again, these processes and the skills which support them are not confined to international management.

It will be clear from this discussion that we are applying a broad definition to HRM, concerned not just with what human resource managers do, but with the skills of people and organizing. On the other hand, there are specific differences between domestic business management and international management which derive from the institutional factors which HRM, the function, has to address. These become apparent when we move from the generic processes of internationalization to country-specific contexts. It is at this point that differences of language, culture, company and employment law, and so forth, begin to loom large. To apply a crude distinction, processes are common, but knowledge is unique.

The attempt to establish a Single European Market (SEM) provides a highly specific context in which to view internationalization. Harmonization and the Social Chapter have begun to highlight the strengths and weaknesses in comparative European systems from which international competitiveness (or the leveraging of domestic advantages) is launched, while rationalization and the encouragement to European companies provides a powerful test of managing across cultural diversity. The final part of the book therefore shifts the focus from generic processes of internationalization and HRM to the specific context of the new Europe.

Chapter 5 considers the impact of the Single European Market on the industrial structure, and what this means for UK firms, given the way the British economy and UK firms are presently

organized. Chapter 6 then reviews the human resource implications for Britain and Europe in terms of three themes – the
consequences for employment and the requirements for skills and
training; the Europeanization of firms and how companies are
responding; and comparative systems of HRM, including the role
of international firms in spreading employment practices. In this
way these two chapters provide specific illustration of leveraging
domestic competitive advantages and coping with issues of
inter-cultural competence.

In summary, then, this book does four things. First, it is
concerned throughout with the similarities and continuities
between domestic and international business management
(although equally we will note areas of real difference which
successful internationalization has to overcome). Second, it
considers the problems of internationalization as they affect both
large and small firms, newly internationalizing firms and mature
international firms – from the first steps through to internationalization in the global firm. This itself is unusual, since most
treatments of HRM in internationalization restrict themselves to
issues in the large, already internationalized, global firm. Third, it
analyses these as generic processes and then with specific
reference to the new Europe. And fourth, it reviews human
resource strategies for internationalization against relevant
theoretical perspectives on the process of internationalization.

This last is also important since such processes underpin what
HRM is called upon to do. At each point, therefore, we outline
relevant theories which explain the what, why, and especially the
how of internationalization. The use of such theories is necessarily
eclectic. This is not a case of HRM borrowing casually from the
strategy literature, as it has sometimes tended to do (as, for
example, in adopting the portfolio concept or modelling the
stages of growth of firms). The reason is that internationalization
itself comes in many forms. As these forms of internationalization
and the processes by which firms arrive there have become more
elaborate over the past forty years, a range of competing theories
have been developed which explain different aspects:

> The sheer variety of transnational activity, however, suggests the
> search for an all-embracing explanation may be illusory.
> Certainly there is no single, universally accepted, theoretical
> explanation of the TNC (transnational corporation). Rather,

there is a variety of competing explanations which operate at different scales of explanation and which derive from different ideological perspectives.

(Dicken, 1992: 120)

Relevant underpinning theories of the internationalization process are therefore introduced throughout the book. These help to highlight the contribution of HRM to international growth by identifying specific behaviours, whereas much of the theory concentrates on the decision to internationalize. (For a systematic presentation and critique of these, the reader is referred to Chapter 3 of Peter McKiernan's (1992) book in this series.)

Within the framework of these four objectives, it is intended that the reader should find a comprehensive as well as critical review of the human resource issues, literature and research relating to internationalization.

Chapter 1

Internationalization and the domestic firm

INTRODUCTION

The treatment of HRM in internationalization has tended to focus on the problems of the large multinational around such issues as the selection, training, and management of expatriates. In part, this reflects particular concerns about the apparently high rate of failure of expatriate assignments within American multinationals. More recently, attention has turned to the problems of coordinating activity and maximizing synergistic benefits in increasingly complex large international companies. Each of these problems reflects a stage in the evolution of large multinationals, especially American ones. Similarly, recent interest within HRM on managing joint ventures and other forms of strategic alliance reflects a feeling within the American business and academic community that they have been somehow asset-stripped (or more bluntly, ripped off) by Japanese rivals with whom they unsuspectingly entered into alliances.

The result of this problem-centred focus is twofold. First, international HRM appears as a series of fragmented responses to distinct and separable problems. Second, it tends to emphasize the disjuncture between doing business domestically and internationally. This blinds us, however, to certain basic similarities and continuities that exist between domestic and international business. If we look more systematically at the different types of issues involved in internationalization, at different stages of internationalization, among both small and large firms, attention shifts from what the HRM function is called on to do to more broadly defined human resource activities and processes. In turn, this serves to highlight continuities with human resource management in the domestic environment in creating an effective organization, and common underlying processes in different aspects of internationalization.

The discipline, theory, and practice of HRM then begins to address issues which are fundamental to the growth of firms internationally, instead of being hooked on the role of the HRM function as an activity following in the train of international business strategies. Identifying human resource continuities and regularities in doing business domestically and internationally does three things:

• it reveals generic processes and skills which are the basis for escaping from the domestic setting;
• it suggests how the domestic environment and analogous settings can be used to develop these skills; and
• it identifies organizational weaknesses which stand in the way of such development.

Since it is typically the difficulties of internationalization which are stressed, identifying commonalities, opportunities, and blocks in relation to the domestic organization and setting can help firms to think more positively about becoming international and to address relevant skills in the present organization.

An overview of internationalization processes suggests there are six areas, or 'contexts', in which there are discernible similarities or regularities with domestic activity and operations:

1 internationalization as the leveraging of domestic competitive advantages;
2 initiating and sustaining international commitment;
3 networking in the newly internationalizing firm;
4 networking and learning in alliances and international joint ventures;
5 managing complexity in the international firm;
6 developing inter-cultural competence.

Each of these 'contexts' defines particular issues for HRM, but also brings out certain key processes that are common across different levels of internationalization – namely, the importance of networking, the role of teams and the goal of organizational learning.

The rest of this chapter provides an overview of these contexts and issues. Succeeding chapters then develop the human resource implications more fully in relation to the different stages of internationalization among small and large firms. As part of this overview, relevant theoretical perspectives on internationalization are also identified. These are developed in greater depth in later chapters.

LEVERAGING DOMESTIC COMPETITIVE ADVANTAGES

Setting aside, for the moment, the scope for large firms to buy their way through acquisition into products, technologies and markets where they are weak and want to be strong, 'going international' is essentially about transferring domestic competitive strengths onto international markets. This is the starting point for the product life cycle approach to internationalization (Vernon, 1966). It is likewise incorporated in Dunning's (1988) 'eclectic paradigm' through the idea of 'ownership-specific advantages'. Thus, internationalization is the process of leveraging domestic competencies in terms of skills into foreign markets and transferring competitive advantages based in such factors as superior technology and products.

In a very simple sense, then, internationalization stems from the domestic operation and the quality of this is therefore of paramount importance. A sidelight on this is that many 'domestic' markets are now also, to all intents and purposes, 'international'. Defending domestic markets means being internationally competitive. In effect, it means having an international strategy even without trading abroad through the need to meet international standards. Thus, internationalization accelerates and widens the competitive arena, unsettling the basis of competition even for domestically oriented firms. This reinforces the argument about HRM needing to attend to the basic human resource strengths of the firm, and where these are below international standards, upgrading them.

In *The Competitive Advantage of Nations*, Porter (1990) takes this as his starting point in arguing that companies require a strong national base. Even globalized firms depend on strong export performance from the home country or on significant outbound export of skills and assets created in the home country. In other words, internationalization depends on domestic strengths. Thus, 'many of the underlying causes of exports and foreign investment prove to be the same', and 'in practice . . . exports and foreign investment tended to occur together' (Porter, 1990: 19, 25).

Just as the quality of a firm's various assets and resources in its home territory matter, so then does the domestic national infrastructure. Basic resource strengths and advantages, including research activity and the quality of human resources, in a nation's localities are fundamental to the ability to compete, whether at home or abroad. Porter's general model (the competitive 'diamond') consequently asserts the importance of domestic systems of education and training for the performance of advanced sectors of industry.

A second feature of Porter's model concerns the impact of industrial specialization at the sectoral and sub-sectoral level, and especially the value of concentration in particular localities. Again, this draws on earlier work, going back to Marshall's concept of 'industrial districts', recent Italian writing on the subject, and Vernon's use of location theory to argue that new products will encourage the development of producers and suppliers in close proximity with customers. Thus, Porter argues that local sectoral specialization will promote innovative and efficient industries (as long as companies operate within an open competitive environment).

This introduces the key theme of networking. A number of Italian writers in particular (for instance, Becattini, 1979; and Brusco, 1989) have explicitly interpreted the strength of 'industrial districts' in terms of network theory. A concentration of advanced firms in the domestic market is a stimulus to innovation, since the richness of industrial networks at home speeds up learning for all firms operating in that market. Moreover, there are clear advantages from participation in a domestic market where many firms operate internationally and lessons for internationalization can be derived indirectly.

A further advantage of this kind of concentration, which bears directly on HRM, is the way it breeds socio-culturally based forms of organization and management systems. Thus, Italian firms in industries like footwear and textiles derive important strengths from the family structures, allegiances and values on which, as networks of small–medium firms, they are based. Such advantages represent 'locked-in' invisible or intangible assets (Itami, 1987; Teece, 1987) which can offset the ready transfer of technology and other kinds of knowledge in the modern world. Such organizational strengths are another example of 'ownership-specific advantages' (Dunning, 1988).

The human resource continuities highlighted here in the leveraging of resources and competencies from the domestic to the international arena are, therefore, skills in the firm and the local labour market, socio-cultural characteristics, and the richness and scope of the firm's networks.

INITIATING AND SUSTAINING INTERNATIONAL COMMITMENT

While the absence of a competitive advantage is an obvious impediment to internationalization, there is a second generic problem which can affect many firms – the existence of blocks to 'thinking international'. Such blocks can prevent firms from taking the first steps, and also prevent companies becoming fully committed to international activity over the long term.

This issue tends to be obscured by the overwhelming tendency of researchers to concentrate on firms actively engaging in internationalization, rather than on those which are not or which have a history of spasmodic overseas ventures. Interviews carried out by the author in a number of medium and large organizations were unusually revealing in this respect, in that interviewees were very clear that elements of their organization structure and human resource systems had made it difficult for them to mount a concerted strategy of internationalization. In other words, the ability to contemplate an internationalization strategy, let alone implement it, cannot be isolated from general organizational and human resource factors already prevailing in the domestic organization.

Such factors include, first, a compartmentalized organization structure in which specialist groups or departments work independently, and where habits of doing things in teams or corporately are weak or undeveloped. In contrast, going international is likely to mean bringing together a range of resources and skills. This tendency to compete rather than to cooperate is reinforced, secondly, by an individualized pay and promotion culture. While international activities may be started by individuals or groups, they are likely to back off as soon as their performance compares unfavourably with that of other groups within an individualistic reward culture.

This, in turn, is reinforced at an individual and corporate level. At the individual level, if the labour market in the industry is very open, with people moving readily between organizations, visible individual performance takes precedence over the corporate activity involved in internationalization. At the corporate level, short-term attitudes to investment and returns will discourage commitment to overseas ventures where effective market entry is likely to take time to establish.

These kind of problems may well reflect specific market factors in the domestic setting where firms are accustomed to compete and on which they have modelled, or against which they have matched, their organization structures and human resource practices. Such problems may well be endemic and common, therefore, to many firms across particular sectors whose forms of HRM and organization have been shaped by domestic business strategies adapted to specific market conditions. Merchant banking would appear to be a case in point.

The issues here relate back to the theme of invisible assets (Itami, 1987), and to seeing organizational strengths (or weaknesses) as 'ownership-specific advantages' (Dunning, 1988) or disadvantages. The leveraging of competitive advantage, in other words, embraces organizational and human resource factors as well as products and technology. Another way of looking at this is that a competitive advantage in terms of product or technology in itself is not sufficient stimulus to internationalize.

Such problems aside, there are also specific human resource difficulties in implementing a decision to internationalize and building an international organization which the newly internationalizing firm is likely to encounter regardless. Chapter 2 will spell these out. In developing an international commitment, therefore, there are both continuities and discontinuities between the domestic and the international that are directly related to formal systems of HRM.

NETWORKING IN THE NEWLY INTERNATIONALIZING FIRM

Entry to a new market, whether foreign or domestic, involves the same basic process of learning about specific customers as a precursor to matching specific operational activities to customer needs and capabilities. This matching process requires considerable knowledge by a supplier and customer about one another, and this implies direct, personal relationships to establish requirements. Network theory elaborates on this by arguing, first, that when firms engage in this way to do business, they exchange resources, and second, that a firm's success at large depends on the richness of its network relationships. A network perspective on internationalization thus stresses exchange processes, social interaction, and the development of long-term relationships between firms.

Network theory begins from the premiss that the individual firm is dependent on resources controlled by other firms, and that it gets access to these external resources through its network positions. These resources are not simply goods and services that are traded, but the knowledge that is employed by the other firms in production, marketing and other activities. For example, supplying a component to another's specification reveals important data about the customer's own product. Similarly, the size and timing of a customer's order gives information about how that customer sees its own markets. Having a full picture of this conversely helps the supplier to determine its own pricing. Such knowledge can be commercially sensitive and as such represents an 'internal asset'. The customer–supplier relationship represents a series of exchanges around these information-based 'internal assets'. Similar information on a wider scale, about other customers and suppliers, enables a firm to build up a broad picture of the market and makes it alive to innovation possibilities.

Networks therefore constitute important 'market assets' through which access is gained to other firms' 'internal assets'. As Johanson and Mattsson (1988: 474) put it, 'the network model direct[s] attention analytically to the investments in internal assets and market assets used for exchange activities'. Such exchange processes are common to both international and domestic business, and involve relationships embodied in people and processes of information exchange.

Stressing the more limited, commonsense view of networks as a 'social web' highlights a second issue – the way in which a firm's domestic network can provide access into overseas networks. Thus, Johanson and Mattsson (1988: 474) assert that 'the firm's positions before the internationalization process begins are of great interest, since they indicate market assets that might influence the process'. In other words, network theory emphasizes the stimulus to internationalization (and to market opportunism in general) from existing domestic networks.

The would-be exporter can learn a lot about foreign markets through its domestic networks of customers, suppliers, and even competitors who have overseas interests. These give a firm indirect access to foreign markets and help define opportunities and restrictions for its own strategic development. More particularly, relations in the domestic market not only provide knowledge, but can act as a driving force to enter foreign markets:

> Market knowledge, including perceptions of market opportunities and problems, is acquired primarily through experience from current business activities in the market. Experiential market knowledge generates business opportunities and is consequently a driving force in the internationalization process.
>
> (Johanson and Vahlne, 1990: 4)

Network theory thus points to continuities between domestic business and internationalization in terms of learning processes and the range of a firm's networks based in people.

NETWORKING AND LEARNING IN ALLIANCES AND INTERNATIONAL JOINT VENTURES

The fourth example centres on what is seen as problematic in managing international joint ventures, and what is the key to their successful management.

International joint ventures were often seen in the past as a way of reducing capital investment, lowering risk, and gaining access to closed markets by linking with an insider. Many firms do still pool resources in this way. The large oil companies, for instance, are each engaged in hundreds of joint projects across the oilfields of the world, to reduce costs, spread risk, and make themselves acceptable to local governments.

Nowadays, however, as Pucik (1988) notes, the rationale is much more related to the speed of technological change and growing competitiveness in global markets. Partners join forces to develop new technologies and/or to take advantage of complementary development skills. In the process, however, the underlying context and motives may remain competitive. Collaboration is simply a temporary and tactical adjustment to market conditions, while the long-term aim of the partners remains to come out on top. Companies in such an alliance are in 'competitive collaboration' (Doz, Hamel and Prahalad, 1986). Collaboration should therefore be viewed as a 'race to learn', the alliance as a transitional stage, and the relationship as a bargain which obsolesces (Hamel, 1991).

There are many factors which affect learning in an alliance. First, and fundamentally, there must be a clear recognition of learning as an objective – a deliberate intent to extract lessons from what the partner does and a strategy to internalize the partner's skills (or 'core competencies'), while also protecting one's own. Beyond this, human resource policies on a wide front can contribute to an effective learning infrastructure. Pucik (1988) identifies various ways in which human resource systems in Western firms fail to provide the basis for effective learning in their joint ventures in Japan. Much of this failure centres on lack of involvement, lack of preparation, and failure to formulate learning as a prime objective. In particular, organization structure and human resource systems and practices, in many Western companies, encourage fragmentation, which leads to a loss of learning.

In contrast, many writers attribute the superior learning ability of Japanese firms to the qualities of teamwork and horizontal and vertical information flow which permeate their organization structures. Teams help to translate individual knowledge, insight and information into collective knowledge by making sure it is shared.

The relevance of information flow and teamwork in the collaborative relationship lies in two related processes. One is the constant pressure of each partner on the other for information, and its exchange through a series of never-ending, daily 'micro-bargains' (Hamel, 1991). The other is the partners' capacity to process and absorb this knowledge. The notion of collaborative exchange as a series of 'micro-bargains' thus stresses the informal aspect of a partnership, rather than the formal terms of agreement. The formal agreement is essentially static, while the race to acquire knowledge and capability is dynamic – depending on personal relationships formed within the alliance and the way information is exchanged on a daily basis.

First, then, learning in international joint ventures depends on teams and habits of coordination, cooperation, and communication bred into the firm domestically. In this respect, the problems of organizational fragmentation and a short-term focus in payment and appraisal systems will be recognizable from the previous section as blocks to internationalization. Second, collaborative exchange once again involves the idea of networking, with its emphasis on personal exchange relationships within inter-organizational settings.

Informal, personal exchange relationships, occurring at numerous points between cooperating firms do not, however, operate in a vacuum. The formal management of human resources determines the basis on which people from one firm interact with those of the other, through the understanding they have of their roles in the alliance, their motivation, and their readiness to learn. A readiness to learn and to seek constant improvements, however, cannot be easily established *de novo* at the time a firm enters into an international joint venture or alliance. It needs to be conditioned over time and to be part of the general climate of the firm.

That apart, formal HRM can contribute at the time through the selection, preparation, and motivation of those individuals who are to play an active part in the alliance, and there are a number of basic practical problems that have to be solved. These include how staff who are assigned to the international joint venture are appraised and by whom, and the protection of careers and benefits (Lorange, 1986).

MANAGING COMPLEXITY IN THE INTERNATIONAL FIRM

The fifth issue is more concerned with the continuities between managing internal and external processes of internationalization, although the means for doing so in both cases are 'ordinary' organizational ones.

Bartlett and Ghoshal (1989) have argued that the challenge facing the modern transnational in essence is to connect resources, innovations, and entrepreneurship which are spread throughout and within the organization. Structural solutions are not sufficent, but require a 'new management mentality'. This involves 'the management of complexity, diversity, and change' (Bartlett and Ghoshal, 1989: 198).

Weick and Van Orden (1990) suggest this has two elements – management through teams, and tackling problems incrementally. The nature of the complexity facing managers in international business is not uncertainty and ignorance arising from lack of information, but too much information that is conflicting, ambiguous and unstructured. They call this 'equivocality' of information. Equivocal problems are made more manageable when the richness of data increases – when views from different perspectives are composed into a meaningful whole. This requires people to pool their views and intepretations, and then resolve differences between them. The forms of communication which score best at this are face-to-face, personalized settings – in other words, teams and small groups.

Small groups and teams also provide the ideal forum for communication on global issues because potentially they can include sufficient internal diversity to match the diversity of the environment they are trying to deal with. The computer theorist, Von Neumann, coined the expression 'requisite variety' to describe this matching process. Networking inside the organization does two things in this respect – it builds the interpersonal relationships on which subsequent team-formation depends, and it digests and filters information through to individuals in a team.

Other considerations are important – such as what makes for an effective working group. Thus, Weick and Van Orden identify relationships based on values of trust, honesty, and mutual respect among members, while others identify common organizational values formed through socialization. Common values provide a 'strong organizational context' (Barham and Oates, 1991) in which trust can flourish, while common socialization develops a basis of tacit and implicit knowledge which can help teams to function more smoothly. In this way, the values, traditions, and common styles of management and leadership that infuse organizational routines are part of a firm's intangible resources (Grant, 1991).

The argument for the importance of teams for sense-making in global management is thus a sophisticated justification for what many others have concluded about the importance of teams to large organizations in general (for example, Kanter, 1989).

The second stage of the argument is about the process for addressing global issues. Because these are characterized by equivocality and uncertainty, it makes sense to tackle issues in small portions, in order 'to create pockets of order' – what Mangham (1978) called 'bite-size chunks', or 'eating your elephant a spoonful at a time'. Incrementalism can result in the accumulation of sequences of successful operational acts of adjustment, from which a sense of the bigger, strategic picture can materialize.

These key skills in the internal management of the global firm, involving teamwork, incremental learning, and networking to manage complexity, are clearly not dissimilar to those in managing the process of internationalization externally. As Bartlett and Ghoshal (1989: 199) note, 'the task of managing across corporate boundaries has much in common with that of managing across national borders'.

Although knowledge relating to different international environments and markets is likely to differ, basic skill development need not differentiate between internal and external internationalization processes. Instead, recognition of these as common and important processes can produce a sharper focus on the elements of skill involved.

Weick and Van Orden list a number of relevant skills which are clearly of wide applicability – for example, negotiation, initiating and managing change, coping with overload, self-management, and understanding organizational politics. The appropriate learning unit for raising awareness and developing these skills is, again, the team.

Weick and Van Orden suggest , however, that process skills in the management of complexity are likely to be highly context-specific, and therefore not readily 'teachable' outside the international firm. Process skills are bound up in the content knowledge of actual situations. This represents an important discontinuity, therefore, between the domestic and the international.

INTER-CULTURAL COMPETENCE

Whether or not boundary-crossing processes are 'internalized' within the firm or not, each carries its particular weight of transaction costs (Buckley and Casson, 1976; Rugman, 1981). Put simply for the moment, that is to say there are gains and losses in efficiency from controlling things entirely within the international firm or, alternatively, leaving them to the market and buying them in. In simple markets, where low-cost production location is the key factor, organizational hierarchy may be a sufficient control mechanism. In complex markets, however, where the basis of competition has shifted towards continuous innovation in the way that Bartlett and Ghoshal (1989) describe, effective teams become an important element in minimizing transaction costs.

Actual transaction costs inside the international firm, however, are not always easy to identify. In one area, nevertheless, they are particularly visible, although rarely considered in this way, and that is in the costs of managing overseas facilities through expatriates. These manifest themselves in such things as pay, travel, and relocation costs. More important still, they show in the failure rate of expatriate assignments, since these directly expose barriers and imply wider operational failures. American firms have experienced particularly high failure rates in expatriate assignments.

Two factors bear especially on expatriate failure or success – one is selection for overseas assignments; the other is preparation through training. A key criterion in each case, whether selecting or developing the individual, is the notion of 'inter-cultural competence'.

The precise meaning of this is somewhat fuzzy. There is a considerable literature which sets out the personality traits and attitudes that relate to adaptability in international settings, but these have proved rather poor predictors of people's success in foreign cultures. One of the more convincing measures of how a person might react is the way they interpret behaviour and evaluate individuals. The readiness to categorize and form fixed judgements ('narrow categorizers'), for instance, is characteristic of a less adaptive, more ethnocentric outlook (Detweiler, 1980; Ratiu, 1983), and therefore likely to cause trouble. This is a quality, one would argue, that is likely to create problems in any setting. Equally, curiosity and openness to ideas are valuable in creating 'global awareness' (Barham and Oates, 1991), but are rooted in a basic outlook and likewise manifest themselves in the domestic setting.

If we turn then to training, while certain skills and knowledge are 'context-specific' and therefore cannot be effectively acquired except on the job, broader inter-cultural competences can be acquired in a variety of domestic settings. Thus, one does not have to cross national borders to acquire cross-cultural experiences (Harris and Harris, 1972). Opportunities abound in countries with diverse religions, racial and ethnic groups, and in the possibilities to mix with groups differentiated by class, age, or sex:

skills for global leadership may be quite generic in application to other management contexts . . . training programmes should attempt to impart generalizable skills by which individuals 'learn how to learn' in any intercultural setting and engage in team building activities with diverse individuals.

(Lobel, 1990: 44)

Just as the desirable qualities to look for in selection, therefore, closely resemble good people skills, so those that training should aim to develop are skills of generic application, not specific to international assignments.

INTERNATIONALIZATION IS DIFFERENT

We have identified, then, six contexts where there are visible continuities between the domestic and international in terms of skills, organizational forms, processes, and issues. These are developed in greater detail through Chapters 2–4. However, it would be naive to suggest that internationalization does not also involve differences, and we have qualified the argument already at a number of points. These include:

1 Working through the immediate domestic network is only sufficient up to a point. Building overseas contacts directly is time-consuming and is a strain particularly for the smaller business.
2 Specific human resource problems have to be surmounted in building an organization for international operations.
3 Formal human resource management has to solve a number of practical problems when employees participate in any joint venture or temporary alliance.
4 Process skills in the management of complexity may be highly context-specific, and therefore not readily 'teachable' outside the international firm or international setting.

In addition, there are a number of other specific discontinuities or differences. For example:

5 The real differences which HRM has to face are not in the internationalization process itself, but institutionally, in such things as recruiting in other national labour markets, accommodating different employment practices, and managing the terms and conditions of expatriates.

6 A particular manifestation of institutional differences is in the way systems of management development are embedded in national labour markets and occupational patterns. As a result, management development systems may lend themselves to particular kinds of internationalization strategy, and be ill-suited to others. As a firm's internationalization strategy matures, therefore, it may require a radical change in management development practices.

Evans, Lank and Farquhar (1989), Evans (1990), and Dulfer (1990), for instance, imply that the functionally-oriented development of specialists in the German system is more adapted to an export-led strategy, whereas the generalist system that is characteristic of Anglo-Saxon, Dutch and Scandinavian firms is particularly suited to transnational operations.

7 Within the process of internationalization itself the biggest obstacle to be overcome is the 'mental maps' managers bring to their understanding of markets and strategic options (Barsoux and Lawrence, 1991). Internationalization means being forced to confront these different mental maps. Such maps are made up of many influences, including:

— detailed knowledge of national markets and consumer tastes and habits;
— assumptions about mission and commitment to product characteristics in which may be embedded a nation's view of itself (for example, Japanese long-termism over technological excellence and return on investment);
— patterns of industry structure which condition perceived strategic options (for example, the localized character of the German beer market).

'Maps' or 'paradigms' can be specific to industries, countries, or to both. The problem is that they are often taken-for-granted understandings, and are therefore relatively impenetrable (Johnson, 1987) – as much for the firm wanting to break out of its domestic market, as for the firm wanting to enter. The ability to change oneself or to innovate in another's market lies, then, with those who can come to terms with what is taken for granted.

These last three 'discontinuities' are all concerned with situationally-specific knowledge, either of the places that internationalization takes an organization into, or of the situations it is coming out of. To an extent, managing these discontinuities is itself all about becoming more aware of what is distinctive in one's domestic national setting. Coping with discontinuities is itself an exercise in 'inter-cultural competence'. Chapters 5 and 6 explore some of these discontinuities through the impact the Single European Market is likely to have on the UK.

SUMMARY

The central theme of this book is that there are many basic continuities and similarities between operating in the domestic and international business environment. These can be described in terms of six contexts for internationalization. These different contexts reveal similarities in processes and the need for certain generic skills. These involve networking, the role of teams, and organizational learning.

Large international firms need to be able to mobilize, within their internal structures, knowledge accumulated in a variety of networks, and to apply these both to new markets and to gain better synergies in existing ones. Newly internationalizing firms need to practise networking skills externally. Firms in alliances need to be able to access knowledge and transfer it through personal exchange relationships. Learning and the use of networks are at the core of all three processes. Such skills are not confined to international management.

In describing these processes, we are clearly applying a broad perspective to HRM, concerned not just with what HRM managers do, but with the skills of people and organizing. Specific differences between domestic business management and international management lie more in the institutional factors which HRM, the function, has to address. Coping with these is itself an exercise in 'inter-cultural competence'.

Chapter 2

Going international

A STAGES APPROACH TO INTERNATIONALIZATION

A considerable body of literature has been concerned with identifying the methods by which a firm can penetrate a foreign market and the reasons for adopting one solution rather than another. Summaries of this literature can be found in Young *et al.* (1989), Dicken (1992) and McKiernan (1992). A basic framework is to consider market entry in terms of three generic methods: exporting, licensing, or foreign direct investment. For each of these there is a variety of sub-types. These include:

- *Exporting*: direct exporting; exporting through an agent; exporting through a distributor.
- *Licensing*: contract sales of knowledge; transfer of rights and responsibilities; sale of brand name, patents, and know how; contract management; franchising; turnkey operations; subcontracting.
- *Foreign direct investment*: assembly; full production or service; greenfield development versus acquisition; wholly-owned subsidiary versus joint venture.

These categories are complicated by a variety of collaborative arrangements between firms, especially with the emergence in recent years of new forms of strategic alliance.

Early attempts to explain the process of internationalization in firms saw it very much in terms of stages. Two such models were Vernon's international product life cycle, and the Uppsala internationalization process model. As evidence and experience accumulated, however, both of these have come to be seen to be dependent on the specific circumstances of the time and place they were describing.

The international product cycle

One of the most influential early models was Vernon's (1966) application of the product life cycle to explain the growth in foreign direct investment (FDI) by American multinationals in Europe and in cheap labour economies. New products will tend to reflect the specific characteristics of demand in local markets. As a high income/high labour cost economy, the United States will therefore tend to encourage the development of labour-saving products. In the early days of such development, new products and the production technology required will be unstandardized and this will favour the close juxtaposition of manufacturers, suppliers, and customers. At this stage, all production is concentrated in the home market and overseas demand (to similar high income markets) is satisfied by exports.

More favourable production costs (for example, cheaper labour) in these initial overseas markets and transportation costs will in due course encourage firms from the home country to set up plants there. Direct threats from local competitors copying the product and/or government tariffs will provide additional stimulus. Production from these sites will displace exports from the home country, and they may also start to export into other, third-country markets, and even back into the original home market. Production economies will encourage further shifts from the more developed countries into ones with lower costs.

The evolution of the world economy and American multinationals since the 1960s caused Vernon (1971, 1979) subsequently to qualify his model. Global multinationals may now develop and produce innovations at any point in their world-wide network, and the simple evolutionary sequence may no longer be realistic.

The Uppsala Internationalization Process Model

Like Vernon's model, the 'Uppsala Internationalization Process Model' rested heavily on observation of how firms had internationalized in one economy at a particular period in time – in this case that of Sweden. Since Swedish firms had a small domestic market, there were considerable pressures on enterprising Swedish firms to internationalize their operations.

Researchers at Uppsala University noted two features of this process in terms of a gradually increasing involvement in foreign markets (Johanson and Widersheim-Paul, 1975). First, firms appeared to move in a series of more or less well-defined stages from exporting to foreign direct investment, to develop fuller involvement and commitment of resources in each particular foreign market (Johanson and Vahlne, 1977). Figure 2.1 illustrates this process of gradual commitment.

Second, in entering subsequent foreign markets, firms were seen to move in an orderly stepwise fashion from those which were closest in 'psychic' (or socio-cultural) distance, to markets that were more 'foreign' and difficult (Hallen and Weidersheim-Paul, 1979). In contrast to Vernon's model, there is more emphasis on

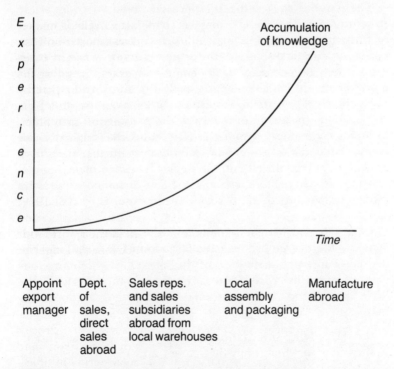

Figure 2.1 Internationalization as a sequential process

finding out about markets, through experiential learning and gradual commitments (Johanson and Mattsson, 1988).

Critics have since argued that this incremental model represents firms at a particular historical juncture, both in their own development and that of markets. For instance,

> [the] experiences of Swedish firms in Japan suggest that establishment and growth strategies on foreign markets are changing towards more direct and rapid entry modes than those implied by theories of gradual and slow internationalization processes.
>
> (Hedlund and Kverneland, 1985: 77)

More recent empirical work bears out this observation. Millington and Bayliss (1990: 159), for example, in a study of fifty large quoted UK firms in the European Community reject 'a narrow incremental view', as do Sullivan and Bauerschmidt (1990) in their study of firms in one sector, in four EC countries.

These studies suggest that it is necessary to take account of the structure of markets, which may be changing. Levels of market maturity and saturation in some industries may have closed off the option of a gradualist approach for new entrants, while in other cases it may be necessary to pre-empt competitors by going for more direct and immediate participation in a foreign market, by some choice of greenfield, acquisition, or joint venture strategies.

A second consideration relates to the maturity of companies. Complex companies operating in different markets may exercise considerable market power and can therefore often pursue more radical (or at least novel) entry strategies. The incremental model may therefore have more relevance to naive (first time) companies internationalizing than to experienced companies (Buckley, 1991).

Johanson and Mattsson summarize the impact of these two factors – the degree of internationalization of the firm, and the degree of internationalization of the market – by defining four types of firm (the 'Early Starter', the 'Lonely International', the 'Late Starter', and the 'International Among Others'), concluding that:

> the [Uppsala] internationalization model is less valid in situations in which both the market and the firm are highly internationalized. The firms which started their

internationalization during the twentieth century were usually in the Early Starter situation. The studies of Swedish firms, on which the Uppsala model is based, describe and explain this situation and its transition to the Lonely International stage. There is no explicit consideration in the model of the internationalization of the firm's environment.

(Johanson and Mattsson 1988: 483)

Many more markets and many more firms are now international in character. Defining the type of market and distinguishing first-time entrants from experienced international firms is therefore important for both analysis and policy. On this basis, the stages model is likely to remain valid for many small–medium enterprises (SMEs). Thus, Buckley, Newbould and Thurwell confirm the orthodox view of 'learning by stages' in their study of forty-three SMEs:

On average, success went to those firms using the longer routes. The inference is that each step gives information to the firm, represents an opportunity for reassessing the overall strategy and forms a base from which the next step can be taken.

As well as success tending to go to those firms using the longer routes, success tends to go to to those firms with more extensive experience of the market; thus those firms with a higher proportion of [export] sales going to the host country tend to have more success with their first overseas production subsidiary in that country.

(Buckley, Newbould and Thurwell, 1988: 66)

This conclusion is of critical importance to a human resource perspective on internationalization because it identifies the role of learning.

THE FIRST STEPS

When a firm first embarks on international trade through export, managers may well perceive this simply as a technical and knowledge problem. They will have specific concerns about getting to know particular markets, setting up distribution channels, regulations and standards they need to meet, export documentation and formalities to be completed, what currency they should trade in, how to deal with exchange rate fluctuations, and so forth. Policy makers concentrate on providing support to firms on such practical matters (through the Small Firm Service, Department of Trade and Industry, and sectoral trade associations), as do a variety of books giving advice (for example, Deschampsneuf, 1988). In many cases, there will be direct training and recruitment implications concerned with specific areas of expertise – for example, on documentation procedures involving clerical staff and, of course, languages.

However, from a human resources point of view, the issues are rather more profound. They centre on the process of learning about specific customers within foreign markets.

Trade does not take place through the operation of price mechanisms alone. It entails the matching of a number of activities to customer needs and capabilities – adapting products and production processes, scheduling, delivery routines, and logistical systems. This requires considerable knowledge by supplier and customer about one another, and implies that the best way to establish these requirements is through direct, personal experience and contact. Recognizing this, industrial marketing puts particular emphasis on buyer–seller relationships. As Webster (1979: 50) argues, 'for strategic purposes, the central focus of industrial marketing should not be on products or markets, broadly defined, but on buyer–seller relationships'.

The importance of the buyer–seller relationship, however, extends beyond the particular character of 'industrial'-type products to marketing generally, and provides a model of inter-firm relationships within internationalization at large. Recognizing the analogies, Swedish researchers have portrayed the development of the business relationship in both industrial marketing and internationalization in terms of network theory (Bridgewater, 1992).

Network theory

Network theory emphasizes exchange processes, social interaction, and the development of long-term relationships between firms. Organizations engage with one another in the first place because few encompass the complete range of supply-chain to-customer resources and activities. As a result, individual firms are dependent on resources controlled by other firms. Such resources are not just tradable goods and services: they embody knowledge. They represent other firms' 'internal assets', in the form of the knowledge they employ in production, marketing and other activities.

Firms get access to the resources that are external to them through their network positions. Networks therefore constitute important 'market assets'. Such networks are dependent on people in the firm forming myriad relationships outside. These relationships have a number of characteristics (Johanson and Mattsson, 1988; Hakansson and Johanson, 1988):

- they are seldom concentrated in one person in each firm;
- they take time to establish;
- they require direct personal contact to discover who has knowledge and influence;
- they are cumulative;
- they are structured by the wider net among firms, with regard to the amount of cooperativeness or competitiveness prevailing;
- they are opaque to outsiders;
- over time they may result in increasing trust and more tightly linked activities;
- this in turn results in a wider system of firms performing interrelated activities;
- while all this points to increasing intensity and stability in inter-firm relationships and networks, the acts of the different parties are also subject to differing interpretations and are therefore susceptible to change.

The network model fills an important gap in the Uppsala model in terms of the dynamics and resources involved in taking the first steps towards internationalization. It also provides a more adequate explanation of firm behaviour in advanced markets. As Johanson and Mattsson argue:

> In the Late Starter situation, we therefore expect the internationalization model to be less valid than the network model because of the importance of indirect international relations in the home market and because of the probably quite heterogeneous pattern of entry opportunities when foreign markets are compared. In the International Among Others case, the internationalization model seems to lose much of its relevance. . . . Since by definition the firm and its counterparts and competitors have positions in a large number of markets,

penetration and integration aspects of internationalization seem to be more important strategic moves than further extension.

(Johanson and Mattsson, 1988: 483–4)

The beginnings of internationalization in smaller firms

The network model enriches appreciation of the first steps in internationalization for smaller firms. Because building relationships and links into foreign markets is time-consuming and potentially hit-and-miss, the conventional solution is to use an agent. An agent provides knowledge of a foreign market, with a minimum of risk and commitment of resources, such as management time. Once potential customers have been located, more direct contacts can be initiated.

The network model, however, draws attention to the learning advantages from participation in a domestic market where many firms operate internationally and lessons can therefore be indirectly derived. The would-be exporter in many sectors can learn a lot about foreign markets through its own domestic networks, where it has existing customers, suppliers, and even competitors with overseas interests. These give a firm indirect access to foreign markets and help define opportunities and restrictions for its own strategic development. This is what is meant by saying that a firm's positions in its domestic network constitute 'intangible market assets' (Johanson and Mattsson, 1988: 476).

Such knowledge, derived from domestic networks, supplements, and ought to precede, the hiring of an agent as a convenient and temporary way to carry out certain tasks overseas. An agent should therefore also be seen as an extension of the firm's own networks, and should similarly be treated as an investment, not simply as handing over responsibility for finding markets.

Many studies of different kinds emphasize the importance of networks generally as a source of learning for small–medium enterprises (SMEs) (Birley, 1985; Thorelli, 1986; Jarillo, 1988; Hendry, Jones, Arthur and Pettigrew, 1991), especially the way in which SMEs' relations with larger customers helps to focus activity and new possibilities (Szarka, 1990; Hendry, Arthur, and Jones, 1991).

A key human resource lesson from all this is therefore:

> Invest in building networks before the internationalization
> process begins, and recognize what can be learnt about
> overseas opportunities through domestic networks.

A firm's relationships in its domestic market not only provide knowledge, but can act as a driving force to enter foreign markets. Examples of this are where a customer adopts an existing supplier when it sets up a subsidiary abroad, or where a domestic customer recommends a supplier to a sister company abroad or to the parent company. In this way, an existing customer acts as a 'bridge' into exporting (Johanson and Vahlne, 1990). From the customer's point of view, 'switching costs' (Porter, 1990) actively favour an existing supplier, because it takes time and money to build up relationships with a new one.

Without this, it is much harder to see how the smaller firm can get started. The existence of a profitable opportunity overseas is an insufficient stimulus because of the difficulty of getting knowledge of such opportunities. Instead, it often requires a strong external 'initiating force' such as a customer, distributor or governmental agency proposing the overseas venture (Aharoni, 1966). Consequently, early ventures into exporting are often fortuitous, rather than planned, and the unsolicited order from a foreign customer is the most consistent reason why firms begin to export (Welch and Wiedersheim-Paul, 1980). Paying attention to building domestic networks is a matter, then, of giving 'happenstance' a chance to do its work.

The following example drawn from a study of SMEs (Hendry, Jones, Arthur and Pettigrew, 1991) illustrates some of these issues and other characteristics of initial exporting. This is one of seven of twenty firms in our study that was exporting – a figure (at 35 per cent of the sample), incidentally, which is close to the national average of 38 per cent of SMEs engaged in exports, reported in a recent large UK survey (Cambridge Small Business Research Centre, 1992).

'Pressings': a case study of a small firm exporting

Pressings is a company of forty-three employees that makes pressed steel housings. Its primary market is in roller conveyor systems for use in the coal industry. Its pressings (called 'idlers') hold the roller shaft, at each end. Its particular innovation has been to incorporate bearings into the housing itself in the form of a prefabricated assembly.

From no exports in 1985, at the time of the study it was exporting 25 per cent of its output by value to the USA, with plans to increase this to over 50 per cent during 1992. Exporting has been crucial to its survival and will be crucial to its growth as the British coal industry declines.

Entry to the US came about through sales to a UK company, which was shipping supplies (at a mark-up) to its American sister company. In 1986, the American company sent technical staff over to see if Pressings could supply direct. A by-product of getting the order was that for the first time Pressings had to lay down effective scheduling procedures.

After delivering the order on time, Pressings received repeat orders and the managing director visited the American firm on three occasions during 1986–8. Meanwhile, development of its revolutionary prefabricated assembly coincided with the American customer's plans for a new product. Samples were exchanged and a larger order followed, as further product upgrading became necessary to satisfy the American end-market.

This series of orders thus gave a toehold in the American market and helped with the development and launch of a new product. It also provided a lifeline without which the company would probably have folded.

Having found they could export to one customer, it seemed obvious it could be done with others. The first step was to get an agent:

How do I find out about what's happening over there? In my view, it's a bit simplistic – you go and have a look. If you can get help in the wings, fine. But you don't have to have an agent. You can find out from consulates, from trade bodies. So you don't *have* to have an agent.

But how do you get an agent? Don't know. So I rang up the Coal Board. They weren't very helpful. So I rang up the Association of British Mining Equipment Manufacturers (ABMEC), because they export over there, and I knew that a helluva lot of management over there, in fact 50 per cent, is British. It so happens I scored a bull's-eye straight away. It's far better to go that route, through the industry itself, than to advertise directly. They put me in touch with somebody in the States, an English bloke who'd emigrated and applied for citizenship. He used to sell mining chain to mining companies all over the world. He's married an American who used to work in the British consulate in Cleveland, Ohio, with specific responsibility for looking after mining manufacturers over there. So a bit of a bull's-eye. I haven't got exactly what I wanted, but I've got 50 per cent. He came and outlined what he proposed to do, acting as an agent for a small number of European manufacturers, so we now have a formal agreement.

(Managing Director, Pressings)

From late 1988 onwards, the agent started to open doors to potential customers, and the Pressings managing director followed this up with a week-long trip in 1988 and four further trips in 1989–90. At £2,000 a time, this commitment represented a lot of money to a small firm. By the time of the study, it had produced one firm additional customer:

So they are on board only a little way, but they are on board, and there are a lot of promising connections. I had a toehold in the US market and I would have been a fool if I hadn't capitalized on that. In Europe, you have the language problem. To give you an idea, the biggest two manufacturers of rollers in the UK each manufacture, in a good month, 130,000 idlers. That's 260,000 of my ends. I've sat and talked with eight to twelve American manufacturers, all of whom each make between 250–300,000 rollers. That's against the backcloth that British Coal in the UK have seven million rollers and mine 100 million tonnes a year [*sic*]. In the States, they mine 1,000 million tonnes a year. Seven million rollers over here; seventy million over there. That's 280 million ends flying around. Ten per cent replacement per annum, that's twenty-eight million. Well, I want a chunk of that. It's that simple. One single major American manufacturer on my tools doubles my turnover, just like that.

I am not saying it is easy, but it is not as difficult as it is made out. This is where a lot of small companies lose out. We deal in dollars, we deal in forward-currency agreements, we invoice in dollars, we are paid in dollars in the United States. So the objective must be to be considered a domestic supplier within the country that you are supplying. This is why we are going to register 'Pressings Inc' in the United States, even if it's only a shell company.

The British have got this terrible reputation. In America they have no qualms about British quality or product design. But they have every misgiving about service, back-up, and delivery.

(Managing Director, Pressings)

Lessons and problems for initial internationalization

The 'Pressings' example provides a number of lessons for initial ventures abroad via export. First, it confirms the importance of networks:

- the active domestic business network is important as a trigger;
- networks, especially information networks, can be complex, comprising many different actors who contribute in different ways.

Knowing how to use and develop networks, however, is a particular gift. But it is one not unassociated with successful managers in general. As Mintzberg's (1973) picture of how managers work indicates, other people provide busy managers with short cuts to essential information. Similarly, Gallo (1988) comments that a key skill in the first stages of internationalization is being able to access and use information. This means being alert to 'hard' data from unconnected sources (such as magazines and economic surveys) and 'soft' data (from the comments of customers, colleagues, or whoever). The skilful user of personal networks can identify and acquire relevant information quickly, efficiently, and cheaply. Identifying useful information itself requires a flexibility of mind (or 'lateral elasticity', as Gallo puts it) which does not prejudge or exclude unsuspected possibilities (such as what markets might be most suitable to tackle first).

Second, there is no substitute for directly engaging with the potential market and customers. Market entry initially depends on this, while longer-term it increases the chances of growth. The aim must be to be seen as a local domestic supplier:

- learning is by doing (as Aristotle observed, the best way to learn how to do something is to go ahead and do it);
- being present in a local (foreign) market gives visibility as well as knowledge of new opportunities.

Personal contacts are especially important in the case of service firms, including those selling design services, since visibility is harder to achieve than if there is a tangible product.

Third, however, there are costs involved. These point to the need before long to broaden the managerial team in the small firm to spread the load, as well as to create a broader network that can be tapped for further growth:

- the development of overseas contacts and information-gathering is time-intensive and imposes severe strains on management, especially in the SME where this activity may depend entirely on the single entrepreneur (Buckley, Newbould and Thurwell, 1988)
- the development of overseas business is founded on mutual knowledge and trust, and a commitment to relationships (another reason why it is time-intensive);
- such activity is a significant opportunity cost in developing foreign business in preference to domestic sales.

Fourth, and finally:

- overseas ventures require confidence and initiative on the part of the entrepreneur.

This last point may seem banal, but is not. It was noticeable in our study of twenty small to medium firms, for example, that all seven that exported had managing directors who had previously worked in larger firms where they had gained experience and confidence in international marketing under more protected circumstances before coming to the SME (Hendry, Jones, Arthur and Pettigrew, 1991). This was true whether they founded the company, took over the family firm from a parent, or were engaged as a professional manager in a private company or subsidiary of a public one. The managing director at Pressings, for example, had come to the company in 1985, on his father's death, after gaining experience of international buying in a large company in the mail-order business – a very different industry.

The issues of confidence and 'learning by doing' are inter-twined. Learning by doing is an important characteristic of initial ventures abroad. As the Pressings example shows, it is very like a voyage of discovery, addressing problems as they arise, making contacts, reframing ideas as knowledge increases. While there are conventional solutions at hand to some of these issues (hiring an agent, contacting the DTI, exploring the Export Credits Guarantee Scheme), the true character of what is involved cannot be easily taught.

Training and support to smaller firms therefore needs to recognize the role of confidence in undertaking such ventures, and especially since much depends on the single entrepreneur, the need to address this in management development activity directed at SMEs. Gill (1988) has made a similar point about training in general for the small business owner. Skill *per se* is insufficient: building confidence to use these skills is required.

Breaking the confidence barrier is one of the most important consequences of an initial venture abroad. This is one of the factors underlying the Uppsala model of gradually increasing foreign commitments, irrespective of learning. Thus, Buckley, Newbould and Thurwell (1988: 177) in their study of first-time investment abroad, further down the track from exporting, make the point that 'confidence was perhaps the main thing to emanate from the first overseas production subsidiary since subsequent ventures were undertaken irrespective of the success of the first'.

This points to a further lesson that 'becoming international' is not just about the decision to go abroad, or how that is implemented. It is also about how the lessons of internationalization are brought home and develop the character of the firm. One of the hidden benefits of an international venture is the knowledge it can give about impending developments in the firm's own domestic market. This was true of a second firm in the study by Hendry, Jones, Arthur and Pettigrew (1991). 'Training International' lost a substantial sum of money in venturing into the US market (arguably because they went straight into opening a US office, before testing out the market in a less committed way). However, in the process the company gained exposure to trends in the market before these started to reach the UK, and was able to prepare itself accordingly. As the managing director observed, 'what has been useful about the US experience is that it has opened our eyes about what is going to happen in Europe'.

For the smaller firm, such learning is arguably absorbed more readily because it is either in one person's head (the entrepreneur's), or it has to be shared with only a limited number of people – hence, the smaller firm's quicker response time. By contrast, institutionalizing learning in the larger firm is a major problem, and we shall consider this in due course.

The major problem for the smaller firm remains one of getting started. Although there are obvious resource issues at all steps along the way, the key to overcoming this, it was suggested, is the extent and character of the firm's networks. Recognizing this fact, much public effort, in the UK and in many other countries, has gone into developing information networks. This, incidentally, is also important in breaking the confidence barrier, by making 'abroad' seem more familiar.

Less attention, however, has been given to increasing the salience of the active business network – in particular, to the knock-on effects of internationalizing part of it. The encouragement of Japanese inward investment into the UK during the 1980s can be seen in this light, although the primary motive was to stimulate changes in UK management and work practices. Equally, attempts to reduce protectionism and open up domestic markets to foreign competition may have a similar indirect effect (as long as this does not wipe out whole sectors and their supply chains).

Targeted efforts to internationalize key sectors as part of a broader policy of stimulating the internationalization of UK firms are less conspicuous. It is not easy to visualize how such a policy might work, and it implies a type of industrial policy not seen for a long time, if ever, in the UK. Nevertheless, a policy to stimulate the internationalization of selected business networks would provide an enriched environment for all firms that come into contact with it.

The background to this argument is the comparative study of the networks of owner-managers in America, Sweden, Italy, and Northern Ireland (Birley, Cromie and Myers, 1990) which draws attention to the problems of small firm networks which are intensive (that is, inward-looking and parochial) rather than extensive (outward-looking with access into other networks, including international ones). It also ties in with Porter's (1990) portrayal of the benefits to innovation and competitiveness from the rich network of links between firms in geographically concentrated sectors.

This discussion of networks brings us back to the character of sectors themselves and how mature, or highly internationalized, they are. In an increasingly internationalized world economy, there are two ways in which networks may affect what Johanson and Mattsson (1988) call the 'Late Starter'.

The positive aspect concerns the process of going abroad. The 'stages model' of internationalization, as we have seen, proposes that entry into first and successive markets will be on the basis of incremental steps into markets that are most like those in which the firm is already operating. This minimizes risk and allows for learning. However, the 'pull' effect of international firms in a network may take the newly internationalizing firm more quickly into more distant markets. This is likely to be an increasing phenomenon as sectors become more highly internationalized.

The negative consideration is that while internationalization among suppliers, customers, and competitors may give the purely domestic firm indirect relationships with foreign networks, and hence access to markets, these networks may already be highly internationalized and tightly linked. Agents and distributers, for example, will already be largely committed to rivals. It will therefore be necessary for the late starter to make direct investment in sales subsidiaries earlier in the process. The resource commitment needed and the lack of opportunity to learn could be serious negatives, both in deterring some firms and increasing the risks.

Highly internationalized 'tight nets' also imply a niche approach. Interestingly, smaller firms may have an advantage in this respect, since small market shares are proportionately more significant for them, while any 'niche' success they achieve may be looked on tolerantly by larger firms already established there. By contrast, large firms trying to break into a foreign market for the first time will be looking for sizeable sales volumes to make the effort and opportunity costs worth their while, and this will entail substantial costs. They will also be more visible to competitors and more unwelcome, and may have to fight harder and longer to gain a foothold. For these reasons, larger firms may prefer to enter via acquisitions or joint ventures to gain a position quickly. Assessing acquisitions and creating joint ventures are problematic, more resource-intensive, and require distinctive skills. Prior experience of doing these things in the domestic market is therefore clearly advisable.

To summarize, the human resource implications for early and late starters are different, but more onerous for larger firms among the late starters. Large-firm late starters will encounter more substantial recruitment and training requirements, and have to bear a higher degree of risk earlier through more adventurous internationalization strategies. Of course, if smaller firms are in direct competition with large firms in fast internationalizing sectors, rather than operating as suppliers or servicing the larger firm, they will equally face significant problems. The underlying problem is then one of size: they simply do not have the resources to compete head-on.

Internationalization and the family enterprise

The issue of size is one that particularly confronts the family firm. The prevalence and role of the family firm in European economies, however, is not widely recognized. Nor, indeed, is the fact that family ownership is not confined to small or even medium-sized businesses.

Drawing on figures for the UK, Germany, and Spain, Welsch (1991), for instance, suggests family firms play a substantial role in Europe. Although there are inconsistencies in the studies he draws on, he estimates family firms are responsible for more than 70 per cent of GNP in Spain and the UK, compared with a figure of 40–50 per cent for the USA (Becker and Tillman, 1978; Dyer, 1986). Other American studies suggest 90 per cent of all firms, including a third of the top 500 Fortune companies, in the USA are family firms (Lansberg, Perrow and Rogolsky, 1988). Whether large or small, however, family firms face particular problems in internationalization. At the same time, these illuminate problems in internationalization for firms generally.

Taking its inspiration from the American Family Firm Institute, the newly-formed Family Business Network (FBN), at IMD (International Institute for Management Development) in Lausanne, Switzerland, under the executive directorship of Professor Alden Lank, has provided a voice for the first time to family firms in Europe. Three problems were expressed by members as the Single European Market approached. First, family firms do not have the necessary networks in other countries to cross national borders in the new Europe – they don't know about trading in other countries, and they don't know the people there, including having access to governments. Second, they are conscious of deficiencies in foreign language skills. And third, as market barriers start to fall, they fear being swallowed up, since, as small firms, they lack the financial clout to resist acquisition by large firms seeking to buy their way into pan-European markets (Alden Lank, personal communication).

These are recognizable as problems for smaller firms generally.

The ultimate threat to survival comes from lack of size, but limited networks are the obstacle to the growth that may overcome this. One way out may be that family firms, and SMEs more generally, will have to learn to form various kinds of alliance to increase their market clout at home and abroad and gain access to foreign markets. Most of the literature on alliances has been from the perspective of large firms, with a focus on equity-sharing joint ventures. Alliances may take a variety of forms, however, and are of increasing interest to smaller firms. This theme is developed in Chapter 3.

Based on studies of firms in Spain and Finland, Gallo and Luostarinen (1991) provide a more systematic review of the issues for family firms. This has an additional interest, however, in revealing some of the basic requirements in internationalization which all firms need to meet. The starting point is that the internationalization process involves change – in products, operations and markets; in systems for information, planning, and control; in organization structure, with new people and responsibilities; and in management attitudes and philosophy. The nature of the family firm creates a number of rigidities which impede necessary adjustments in these areas. On the other hand, the family firm also has certain advantages which can make it more flexible in internationalization than other firms.

First, internationalization implies growth, but the owner(s) of the archetypal family firm (as studies of SMEs generally have suggested) may be looking just to provide themselves with a steady living and want to keep the firm at a size they can adequately control (Bolton Report, 1971; Stanworth and Gray, 1991). They may be risk-averse. It may also mean adapting products or services to different kinds of customer. Not only does this go against the grain of what is likely to have been a localized, niche-oriented business (Hendry, Arthur and Jones, 1991), but it also involves additional resources which its 'closed' form of ownership may make it difficult to generate without surrendering some control. On the other hand, the family firm is more likely to be oriented to the longer term than public companies who have to satisfy shareholders.

Associated with this is a second issue of culture, whereby the family business is often closely bound up with the locality and local interests. This can restrict horizons.

Third, internationalization means elaborating the organization structure and possibly admitting outsiders into senior positions. This threatens patterns of status, power, and control within the family firm, including information systems which are often informal, direct and personal, and centred on the head of the family. Against this, the high degree of focus in control and decision making provides the strong management which the newly-internationalizing firm is likely to need to see it through difficulties. Gallo and Luostarinen (1991) also point out that family firms often segment their operations in the second generation to give family members their own business unit to run. This makes it easier to create and resource an international business.

A fourth problem, however, is that inter-generational family dynamics, coupled with the strategic perspective of an older generation, may mean internationalization is only possible through a complete generational change. A member may be allowed to 'play' with internationalization up to a point, without being given adequate resources to make it work successfully.

Finally, since the family firm is more inward-looking and dependent on its own human resources to a greater degree than firms generally, its international perspective is dependent on the experiences and attitudes of family members. The interest of family firm owners in the development of their children to take over the business, however, may make them more attentive nowadays to their offspring getting experience overseas, while opportunities for social travel are likely to feed back directly into the family's business horizons.

One thing especially that these observations do is to emphasize that internationalization is a 'social process' (Hymer, 1976) which challenges attitudes to risk, patterns of power and control, and organizational culture. Overcoming or confronting these is a human resource issue centred on learning. The final section in this chapter develops this theme, drawing on some original case material featuring large firms.

BLOCKS TO INTERNATIONALIZATION

'Going international' is about exporting, licensing, and the first steps in foreign direct investment. It is also, however, about overcoming blocks to thinking international. Such blocks can afflict firms on first starting out, but equally can prevent companies becoming fully committed to international activity. The result can be seen in spasmodic overseas ventures. This problem of thinking international, and especially its origins, is not well recognized.

While preceding sections largely focused on active steps towards developing international business, we take a step back here to identify two kinds of blocks to internationalization. First, there are blocks simply to 'thinking international'; second, there are the difficulties in actually putting into place a decision to internationalize. These problems concern larger firms as much as smaller ones, perhaps more so since there is a greater inertia (or mass) of organization and established ways of thinking to overcome.

Thinking international

We have stressed from the outset the continuities between domestic activity and internationalization. Thus, internationalization cannot be seen in isolation from a firm's broader strategy. It is only one option in any policy for the growth of a firm (Luostarinen, 1979). As Rosenfeld, Whipp and Pettigrew (1989: 25) observe, 'A jarring note in many studies of internationalization is the assumption that it can be isolated from the rest of an organization's strategy.'

The external environment and how managers read it is critical to their interest in internationalization. If overseas markets are regarded as difficult or specialized, while the domestic market is protected, there may be every justification for avoiding overseas activity. Many sectors, for instance, remain fragmented or regulated, and world-wide are divided into multiple domestic markets (Porter, 1990).

The process of market entry can also affect commitment (notwithstanding also the legitimate tactic of exiting from a market). Internationalization, for instance, may not involve a conscious strategic decision and a willingness to commit resources long-term. As the 'Pressings' case showed, going abroad may be fortuitous, through the role played by existing customers in the firm's network. If an opportunity briefly presented then begins to recede and no effort is made to actively explore or develop the market, the export interest may be short-lived. The same effect can arise when the strategy has not been a corporate one, but depends on an individual champion.

A good illustration of these processes is the case of Kleinwort

Benson in merchant banking, cited in Rosenfeld, Whipp and Pettigrew (1989). After the international financial relationships built up by Kleinwort & Sons had been destroyed by the Second World War, Kleinwort shifted its focus to opportunities in the domestic market. In the 1960s, the newly formed Kleinwort Benson developed overseas lending and opened representative offices, largely at the request of established clients as exchange controls were relaxed. In the 1970s, ventures into overseas markets, such as Japan, were undertaken because of the enthusiasm of individual directors. However, without sustained corporate commitment such ventures were always liable to be prematurely abandoned whenever strong competition emerged. Only in the 1980s has Kleinwort Benson developed a proper global perspective on its business – through a combination of factors, involving political, regulatory, technological, and leadership changes. An important element making this reorientation possible was the restructuring of the organization around the three main business areas. Similar patterns can be found elsewhere in merchant banking, where fragmentation and regulation have encouraged a halting approach to internationalization.

An important contributory factor to such behaviour is the way in which organization structures and systems themselves make it difficult for companies to mount a concerted strategy of internationalization. The ability of firms to contemplate an internationalization strategy, let alone implement it, cannot, in other words, be isolated from general organizational factors. These include organizational structure and the human resource systems embedded in it. Organizational systems can create blocks simply to 'thinking international'. In this way, many firms are held back even from getting to the starting line.

A number of related issues of this kind were identified by the author in interviews carried out with seven large organizations in a project for the Department of Employment (Hendry and Pettigrew, 1992). Four of these are described:

1   Going international is likely to mean bringing together a range of resources and skills and focusing activity through teams. If an organization does not habitually do this, but has groups of specialists working independently, it has difficulty starting or sustaining international activity. A compartmentalized organization structure is therefore a major impediment.

2 If groups and individuals are rewarded through pay and promotion also on an individualistic basis, they are likely to compete rather than cooperate. International activities may be started by individuals or groups independently, but they are likely to back off as soon as performance compares unfavourably with that of other groups in an individualistic reward culture. An individualized pay and promotion culture is therefore a second problem.

3 If the labour market in the industry is also very open, with people moving readily between organizations, visible individual performance takes precedence over the corporate activity involved in internationalization. The external labour market can therefore reinforce the effects of an individualized reward system.

4 Finally, if an organization is dominated by short-term perspectives on investment and returns in its domestic activities, it is likely to be unwilling to sustain commitment to an overseas venture where effective market entry may take time. At the first sign of difficulty, it is likely to withdraw. This is a major underlying problem with companies, and potentially with whole economies, where short-term attitudes to investment prevail.

Again, merchant banking is characterized by many of these features. Activities are highly specialized, in markets having very different profiles; there is little movement of people between them, and they are managed in a compartmentalized way; overseas initiatives are pursued on a case-by-case basis, and driven by individual executives; there is a strong individual performance culture, and people relate to the external labour market for their specialist areas; finally, the preoccupation with risk and its minimization, coupled with the high visibility of profit- and loss-making activities, produces lack of sustained commitment to markets.

Problems in implementing a decision to internationalize

Even with commitment and no underlying obstacles, building an organization for international activity presents a number of distinct human resource problems. Whereas the previous examples show internationalization problems rooted in the domestic organization, the ones here mostly reflect qualitative differences between doing business internationally and domestically. Special problems in building an international business include:

- a lack of people initially with international experience, and a lack of sufficient and suitable international business to develop such experience;
- staffing international activity without taking the best people from valuable domestic operations;
- defining the skills for internationalization when the form it will take, the shape of the market, and the precise nature of the product or service for it may be unclear – in other words, having a model of what internationalization in the particular sector should look like;
- determining the scope of internationalization in the organization and therefore who needs to think international.

In addition, internationalization puts a strain on the management development and career pathing system, which may, in any case, be inadequate even for domestic purposes. If that is so, it will certainly be ill-adapted to the requirements of internationalization to have more rounded 'general managers'.

Looking at these in more detail, the first problem is that there is likely to be a scarcity of people with relevant skills, and limited opportunities to develop them inside the organization. The conundrum is how to develop international managers in advance of having any suitable international business to manage. In this respect, internationalizing is in fact no different from entering any new market. It is made more difficult, however, when the international market itself is in the process of forming, and its shape and the timing of entry is uncertain.

The European life assurance market is at present at this stage, with national regulations still a factor. One route is to place existing staff in embryonic businesses in the relevant foreign markets, to become acquainted with language, culture, rules of business, and the way the markets work locally. However, such businesses need to be 'real' businesses for the exercise to be developmental (and financially justifiable). An alternative is to recruit non-UK nationals from the countries in question who have some experience of those markets, or at least of language and culture, and bring them into UK operations to learn the parent business. The latter assumes acculturization into the business is easier than into the ways of the country. A combination of both can start to build an international resource base, sufficient for initial purposes.

The second problem is that staffing international activity may take the best people from valuable domestic operations. Should an organization take its best, most experienced people, probably from activities that are highly valued and a source of profit? If so, there may be significant opportunity costs in resourcing initial ventures. One solution is not to use established staff, but relative newcomers. Newcomers are likely to be more natural 'product champions' for new ventures, since they have a reputation to make, not one to lose.

Alternatively, there may be other parts of the organization which already have an international presence, that the newly internationalizing operation can 'net' into. A business like ICI Acrylics has been able to set up plants in Europe where other ICI divisions already had site management in place. This reduces overheads, but more importantly provides a ready-made and experienced service and administrative structure.

Third, it is difficult to define the skills for internationalization when the form it will take, the shape of the market, and the precise nature of the product or service is unclear – in other words, there may be no model of what internationalization in the particular sector should look like. When an organization goes international, the market is new to it, whether or not others understand it. A common problem is that skills are by definition unclear, in short supply, and often more complex. If the market itself is only just becoming more international, there is also no clear model for the firm to follow, and skills are likely to be in short supply in the external labour market.

The telecommunications market is at this stage, internationalization schemes hitherto having consisted of consortia arrangements to lay cables or launch satellites, a host of bilateral agreements to exchange payments for international telecommunications traffic, and highly regulated domestic markets. One choice for further internationalization is to provide the whole range of telecommunications services as a package to business customers who are themselves international and need large, protected communications networks. This has the advantage of being relatively invisible to competitors, especially when initially focused on a few customers to solve technical problems and establish standards. The structure for implementing this is likely to combine market-oriented business divisions and various specialist groups, in project teams. In skill terms, it means bringing together many esoteric technical skills, developing hybrids of these, and infusing engineers with a commercial and marketing orientation. Such hybrid skills and competences, however, are likely to be in short supply.

The fourth issue is to do with the scope of internationalization and the fact that many people in an organization may need to think international. In telecommunications, internationalization can be largely managed through technology, with relatively little impact on the domestic operation and the majority of the staff. In other kinds of organization, however, it may be important that many more people see internationalization touching on them and their work.

If, for example, the majority of employees see themselves concerned only with domestic markets, there may be divisions between them and international 'product champions'. This can surface in tangible form in the reluctance of production, product development, service, and marketing staff to provide customized product, in small quantities, with adequate support to overseas markets, as a precursor to larger volumes. Therefore, all employees may need to 'think international' – not just those who regularly engage with overseas markets.

Firms can tackle such problems of awareness in all sorts of ways – from the symbolism of flying international flags, to the practicalities of giving all staff some basic foreign language expressions relevant to their tasks. This is important, for instance, for those like secretaries and catering staff who routinely come into contact with visitors.

The fifth problem in implementing internationalization is the suitability of existing management development and career pathing for internationalization. The internationalized firm needs to develop sufficient people on a continuing basis through a variety of functions, businesses, and countries. As international activity grows, this will tend to acquire momentum. In the early days, however, the company is likely to lack a sufficient critical mass of international jobs and people to manage movements of staff in and out of domestic and international operations smoothly and effectively. Unless actively planned, this is a recipe for disillusionment among those who are taken out of domestic posts to undertake international assignments, only to find that their re-entry into commensurate posts at home is blocked.

Some organizations may lack the rudiments of a decent management development system to start with, even for domestic purposes. It will be doubly difficult for them to meet international staffing requirements. On the other hand, internationalization may provide the trigger for a long-needed overhaul of their systems. There may be an additional complication that a management development and career system that works domestically may be a weakness when internationalizing. One that is geared to developing people up functional ladders will not be producing rounded general managers sufficiently early in their careers to take on international assignments.

The fully internationalized firm has to address some of these issues as continuing problems. But for those taking their first steps towards international activity, they present special obstacles.

CONCLUSION

In this chapter we have looked at internationalization in terms of the first steps the newly internationalizing firm needs to take. In keeping with the underlying argument of the book, we have identified the similarities and continuities that exist between domestic and international business, and which can be used to propel a firm into international activity. These centre on the themes of networking and learning. More specifically, they concern the processes of information-gathering and assimilation through networks, and of adapting to the requirements of foreign markets.

In one sense, internationalization is about leveraging resources and competencies from the domestic into the international arena. This requires many kinds of adjustment, however. Internationalization is not a process simply of transferring domestic strengths, but of adapting product functionalities, technologies, and marketing approaches to situations which are subtly and sometimes substantially different (Abell, 1980). It begins in learning about specific customers in other markets, but is likely then to require change in accustomed ways of doing things domestically.

From looking at the steps firms take to internationalize, we therefore turned to the organizational weaknesses which stand in the way of such development. These included blocks to thinking internationally and specific changes that have to be made in the domestic organization to implement an international commitment.

Human resource management in its formal, functional sense has a role to play in undoing blocks and assisting implementation. More broadly, however, its relevance lies in the fact that internationalization is a 'social process'. Networking is a social skill, while organizational phenomena such as attitudes to risk, patterns of power and control, and culture are fundamentally social in character. Overcoming or confronting problems of this kind which inhibit internationalization is a human resource issue centred on learning.

Chapter 3

The role of alliances in internationalization

ALLIANCES: A HALF-WAY HOUSE OR A THIRD WAY?

One of the central concerns in the analysis of internationalization has been the point at which, and the reasons why, firms switch from exporting to making foreign direct investments (FDI). In the course of this transition, they may also make use of intermediate tactics such as licensing. Different literatures and perspectives tend to emphasize certain options and neglect others. For instance, the international marketing literature has tended to neglect FDI by concentrating on export processes, while the product life cycle formula neglected licensing. To redress this, various writers sought to specify the timing of the switch from export to foreign direct investment, and the conditions under which licensing might be a preferred option (Buckley and Davies, 1980; Buckley and Casson, 1981).

At the same time, the rapid growth in collaborative arrangements between large multinationals in the 1980s triggered an interest in the general phenomenon of strategic alliances. These take many forms, and include a number of arrangements traditionally described under both licensing and FDI. The difficulty of making such alliances work, however, and the tendency of joint ventures, for example, to fall apart, has generally given them a bad press (Harrigan, 1986).

Nevertheless, alliances remain an intriguing phenomenon, especially those which fall short of full equity deals. Because non-equity forms of alliance tend to be confined to specific functions or kinds of activity (Dicken, 1992; Business International, 1987), they are less visible and it is easy then to underestimate their prevalence and significance. At the same time they are more focused, potentially short-lived (maybe intentionally so), have both competitive and cooperative features, and are likely to actively involve employees from participating organizations. As such, they depend on both intra- and extra-organizational networking processes.

For smaller firms, alliances can provide a way in to foreign markets by overcoming their limitations of size. For larger firms that already have an international presence, alliances are a way of coping with increasingly complex global markets. In between, there are those medium-to-large domestic firms which are in a sense forced on to the international stage by the entry into their own domain of even larger foreign firms (Lyons, 1991). As small fry internationally, they may look to alliances as a defensive manoeuvre.

This chapter looks at the role of alliances in assisting (and defending against) internationalization among small, medium, and large firms. Once again, we place this in the context of relevant theories of the internationalization process and identify continuities with domestic activity. Insofar as alliances can be formed equally with domestic as with foreign firms, such continuities are self-evident. More interesting and to the point is the way in which building and sustaining alliances through networking and teams is a 'normal' organizational process independent of alliance activity.

Transaction costs and the theory of 'internalization'

The decision to switch from exporting to foreign direct investment is governed by locational considerations (such as transport costs) and whether to 'internalize' more of the trading process within the structure of the firm by setting up sales and eventually production facilities in the foreign market. This process of 'internalization' is based on the trade-off between controlling resources within the firm against the costs and risks of committing resources in order to extend the physical boundaries of the firm.

Transaction cost theory addresses this problem by paying particular attention to the difficulties of pricing the know-how of agents (individuals or firms) and controlling the performance of contracts with them (Williamson, 1975; Rugman, 1981; Dunning, 1981). These difficulties are especially acute in contractual relationships like licensing which involve the trading of knowledge. The licensee will be at a disadvantage in agreeing the price, but the licensor runs the risk of losing control of its know-how and/or incurring policing costs to make sure any restrictions on the terms of the license are adhered to. The difficulties involved help to account for the development of multinationals because they bring these transactions within the hierarchical control of the organization (Rugman, 1986). On the other hand, organization costs are then incurred.

The overall aim will be to minimize costs (hence, the full description, 'the transaction cost minimization theory of internationalization'). Initially, exporting involves a lesser commitment of resources of capital and people, but leaves direct responsibility for the selling process at a distance, with agents or isolated overseas sales staff. At this point, the organization costs of acquiring market knowledge in-house and bearing the full risks of external uncertainties such as political instability outweigh the transaction costs of managing across organizational boundaries and the potential for the agent to capitalize on knowledge and opportunities gained (Anderson and Gatignon, 1986). As sales increase, market knowledge and political contacts become more certain, adverse locational costs increase, and the risks of losing competitive know-how become greater. The result will be direct investment in the foreign market.

In between, transaction cost theory explains why licensing is invariably a least-preferred option. The reason is the high transaction costs involved in designing and maintaining contracts governing the formation and use of a license (Buckley and Davies, 1980). As already noted, these include the costs of circumscribing the rights in the technology that the licensee enjoys and policing these, along with the risk of creating a competitor. In consequence, licensing accounts for only 7 per cent of total foreign sales by British companies (Buckley and Prescott, 1989), with a similar proportion in other trading nations.

One of the best-known examples of successful licensing involves the St Helens' glass company, Pilkington. By licensing its revolutionary 'float glass' method of manufacture, it used the resulting income stream, of £425 million over 25 years, to transform itself into the largest producer in the world. Since bulk transport of glass was not then feasible and therefore precluded export, the company judged that the alternative of building plants outside the UK was beyond its resources and the cost of protecting its patents would also be considerable and probably unavailing. Instead, by licensing, the company generated funds that enabled it to build plants in relatively undeveloped markets (Sweden, Australia, Canada, Mexico, South Africa) from which the terms of its licenses excluded competitors, and then to acquire major companies in the developed world's heartland markets (the USA and Germany). In the meantime, however, its rivals acquired the technology and have remained a direct competitive threat, while also depressing profits through the excess capacity the industry has tended to create (see Hendry and Pettigrew, 1989).

Like licensing, alliances represent a kind of 'half-way house', with similar problems in protecting a company's knowledge, or 'intangible' assets.

Although it tends to be couched in rather abstract economic language, the relevance of transaction cost theory to human resource management is its focus on exchange relationships in internationalization, and on specific behavioural processes such as bargaining, information-exchange, and controlling contracts. Although concerned primarily with pricing these, it draws attention to issues of 'cheating' and 'shirking' in trying to manage these through open market relationships, as well as to the way organizations try to reduce these problems through hierarchical systems and relationships.

Methods of foreign market servicing

The general model offered by transaction cost theory needs, however, to be supplemented by a more detailed view of what exactly may be externalized or internalized. Buckley, Pass and Prescott (1990a), for instance, have argued that internationalization in relation to any single market is not unidimensional, but involves a variety of activities within the firm. They call this 'channel management', rather as Porter (1980) refers to the 'value chain'. Building on Buckley and Casson (1976), they argue that:

the categorization of foreign market servicing strategies [that is, ways of serving foreign markets] into exporting, licensing and foreign investment is too crude a division because it ignores the crucial role of channel management. Marketing costs cannot simply be aggregated as a lump: costs of distribution, stockholding, transport, promotion, retailing and generating new customers are radically different.

(Buckley, Pass and Prescott, 1990a: 38)

Each element of the total marketing activity in consequence is susceptible to different levels and kinds of internationalization in where it is located and who controls it.

Choices about channel management have implications for specific technical competences (or knowledge and skills) a firm needs to acquire, for information flows between them, and for management's ability to control relevant competences inside and outside the firm. Relationships between 'channel' activities and the flow of information are critical and a vital source of competitive advantage (Buckley *et al*, 1990a), while relatively minor adjustments in channel management strategies can improve the competitiveness of firms (Buckley, Pass and Prescott, 1990b). Similar considerations to do with information flow apply to the activity of entire functions across the firm – especially to relationships between research and development, production, and marketing.

What the channel management and value chain concepts do, in the present context, is to draw attention to the range of issues an alliance, even one confined to marketing, may have to address, and the variety of forms alliances may take. It provides an antidote to the over-simplistic representation of externalized market relationships in transaction cost theory.

Alliances as networks

The question is, then, 'are alliances a half-way house or a third way?' Even the highly globalized firm (especially the highly globalized firm?) operates through externalized networks. These are both diverse and dynamic (Dicken, 1992). As Dicken points out:

What is new is their current scale, proliferation, and the fact that they have become *central* to the global strategies of many firms rather than peripheral to them. Most strikingly, the overwhelming majority of strategic alliances are between competitors. Of 839 agreements identified by Morris and Hergert (1987) between 1975 and 1986, 81 per cent were between two firms and no less than 71 per cent were between two companies in the same market.

(Dicken, 1992: 213)

Moreover, many companies are forming not single, but multiple networks of alliances. A recent newspaper report provides a good illustration of this. The report is also interesting from a human resources point of view because it shows the importance of interlocking directorships as a mechanism for framing alliances and as a channel for mutual learning about markets. At the same time, it presents a contrasting use of alliances in joint bidding for projects. It thus illustrates two very different uses of alliances, about which we will say more later – alliances as a vehicle for learning in pre-competitive situations, and alliances as a way of pooling resources (and satisfying political interests).

PowerGen looks to Europe

Ed Wallis, chief executive of PowerGen, last night forecast expanding international opportunities in partnership with some of Europe's leading electricity companies, following his appointment to the international advisory board of the German utility, RWE.

Mr Wallis joins Jean Bergougnoux, chief executive of Electricité de France, and Heinrich von Pierer, who is set to take over as head of the Siemens advisory board next October, on the 20-strong RWE advisory board. RWE is one of Germany's leading electricity utilities and controls the national grid.

Mr Wallis said his appointment reflected RWE's desire to learn about the competitive UK electricity market established through privatisation, at a time when Europe was becoming increasingly competitive. But RWE was also looking for business partners around the world, he said.

RWE is one of three German companies joining forces to renew the ageing electricity infrastructure in east Germany, in partnership with Preussen Elektra and Bayernwerke. They would share 85 per cent of the project, but EDF is hoping to take a 7.5 per cent stake, with the remaining 7.5 per cent shared between PowerGen, Electrabel of Belgium, Endesa of Spain and possibly Enel of Italy.

However, the plans are thought to be making slow progress. Mr Wallis said there were opportunities in east Germany and elsewhere, but PowerGen's immediate concern was Portugal, where it was bidding for two power station contracts.

It is part of a consortium, headed by Siemens, to build a Combined Cycle Gas Turbine plant at Tapada do Outeiro, near Oporto, for the Portuguese utility, EDP. The project, being negotiated with the government, is valued at £320 million.

(Simon Beavis, business correspondent, *The Guardian*, 16 November 1991)

Network theorists have argued that the highly internationalized firm has a greater choice in externalizing activities because it can access linked networks (inside and outside the firm) and wields greater market power. It can therefore take a more relaxed view of what it controls inside, without the risk of losing control of crucial internal assets. The network model thus challenges the presumption that international firms will tend towards increasing internalization of market relations.

Moreover, unlike the 'internalization' model, it emphasizes the gradual development of market knowledge, rather than the simple need to exploit and protect internally created intangible assets. As Johanson and Mattsson (1988: 483) argue, 'the [internalization] approach does not consider the cumulative nature of activities, the use of external assets, the development potential of network relationships, or the interdependence between national markets'.

It is this latter – the developmental possibilities of networks – that we now focus on. The use of networks to help the firm develop is highly relevant in cooperation between smaller firms and also for the formation of strategic alliances in environments which are more highly internationalized.

COOPERATION AND STRATEGIC ALLIANCES AMONG SMALL–MEDIUM ENTERPRISES

A recent survey of small to medium firms in the UK concluded that 'collaborative arrangements may thus be an important – possibly increasingly important – element in the growth and competitiveness of SMEs, especially in the relatively dynamic professional and business service sector' (Cambridge Small Business Research Centre, 1992). First, the study shows the importance of formal networking of all kinds – just under a third of 2,028 firms surveyed (32 per cent) having formed some kind of collaboration with other organizations. This includes links with higher education (4 per cent of all SMEs).

Second, it shows considerable collaboration with customers (12.5 per cent) and suppliers (12.4 per cent). Backward and forward links of this kind may not be unexpected, given the close association which many smaller firms forge with larger firms in the course of developing niche positions (Hendry, Arthur and Jones, work in progress). Third, and perhaps least expected, is the degree of collaboration with competitors (5.4 per cent) and with firms having complementary interests (5.3 per cent).

The three most important reasons cited in the survey for forming these links are to expand their range of expertise or products, to assist in the development of specialist services or products required by customers, and to provide access to new UK markets. In other words, all of these (along with others mentioned, such as sharing R&D costs) are ways of increasing the scale and scope of their operations without losing their independence in full mergers. The fourth most common reason is to directly assist in gaining access to overseas markets (mentioned by 14.8 per cent of all firms). However, as we have consistently argued, any strengthening in domestic competitiveness also has an international dimension.

These two processes go hand in hand, and perhaps need to take place sequentially – strengthening the domestic base (through alliances) and then developing international alliances. As Jarillo and Martinez (1990) argue:

> Most [SMEs] do not have the necessary resources to compete across the full spectrum of activities of the value chain, while obtaining the full economies of scale necessary to remain competitive. The process of unification of European markets is leading to an increase in the minimum efficient scale . . . . This leaves SMEs with a set of hard choices: facing the need to suddenly grow in size, they can either merge with other companies, preferably across borders (something very rarely achieved with a minimum of success); sell out to larger firms; or try to achieve the necessary scale by specializing in a few steps of the value chain and then creating networking arrangements with other firms across Europe to take care of the rest.
>
> (Jarillo and Martinez, 1990: 17)

Experience in developing networks within Europe provides some illustration of this. It suggests the initial focus should be on local networks to strengthen competitiveness, before going wider afield.

Certainly, international alliances ought to stand more chance of success if a firm has already acquired some experience of them in the home country. Since surveys indicate that the majority of SMEs – in France, in Germany, and in Britain – did not expect to be affected by the Single European Market and were not making particular preparations for it (Berney, 1990), European-wide initiatives are not likely to make as much impact at this point as domestically-focused initiatives.

Alliances within countries

At national level, a number of countries have active programmes to encourage networking and cooperation among SMEs. Denmark, for example, in 1989 committed 150 million kroner (approximately £15m.) 'to encourage network cooperation among SMEs' (Nielsen, 1989), based on fairly well-established cooperative experiences in the Danish economy and successful network practices in the USA, Italy and Germany. The features of intended 'cooperation' among Danish SMEs are instructive:

1 [The programme] is concerned with independent small companies. Networks are not mergers, on the contrary they are cooperation schemes which capitalize on the strength of the independent, competitive and flexible small company with the objective of compensating for some of its weaknesses.
2 The definition is not formal – it says nothing about the legal framework, number of companies, size of companies, what they are cooperating on, whether they are in the same branch or different branches [of business] or any such matter . . . .
3 The real objective of the programme is stated in the phrase 'to compete successfully with the best of the large companies' . . . . Only when [companies'] cooperation specifically aims at new business opportunities, new markets or a new competitive edge is it considered a network.

(Nielsen, 1989: 2)

The programme combines measures to do with education and training (aimed at company managers and employees, public bodies, business consultants, and various other 'brokers'), financial incentives, and information dissemination.

Thus, it is directed at networking among Danish firms inside Danish borders to strengthen them competitively. As Nielsen

(1989:1) observes, the objective is 'enhancing the international competitiveness of Danish industry', whether they seek to trade overseas or simply defend their domestic market. This is a critical point in any discussion of internationalization, and one we keep returning to:

> Internationalization is about competing effectively in international markets. Many 'domestic' markets, however, are now, to all intents and purposes, 'international' (especially those within the Single European Market of the European Community). Defending domestic markets means being internationally competitive and may mean having an (international) strategy to ward off international competitors.
>
> Conversely, 'going international' is about translating domestic competitive strengths on to international markets, or, if these are weak in terms of skills, technology, or other kinds of resources, upgrading them and, if necessary, using alliances to compensate for weaknesses and increase the scale of resources available to the firm.

In addressing firms' underlying international competitiveness, the Danish programme aims 'to create, maintain, develop, and renew core skills' (Jakobsen and Martinussen, 1991). Thus, the network approach here recognizes the high degree of specialization which often characterizes SMEs (Hendry, Arthur and Jones, 1991), and seeks both to exploit this by reinforcing core skills and to compensate for the deficiencies which typically accompany over-specialization:

Two aspects of this kind of network cooperation are important:

- The more specialised the production is, the larger geographical markets have to be addressed. Consequently, the company has to establish relations to more companies, even though these are 'only' exchange network relations.
- When companies specialise they tend to have insufficient interface competence needed for joining the network cooperation, and therefore show increased needs for use of external resources, such as external consultants or other companies.

(Jakobsen and Martinussen, 1991: 5)

In other words, through specialization, SMEs' networks and internal resources become over-focused and truncated, and 'breaking out' is problematic and difficult (Hendry, Arthur and Jones, 1991).

In the two years to mid-1991, the Danish programme received expressions of interest to form networks from around a third of Denmark's 7,500 SMEs; eighty networks were in the implementation phase (after feasibility studies), with expectations that another 150 would eventually join them; and 89 per cent of applications had come from firms with less than 100 employees. Jakobsen and Martinussen comment that, 'in many cases the networks address export markets, which is not possible for the companies individually', and that 'the employment and export by these network companies will be considerable within 5–10 years'. The success of the programme has attracted interest from a wide range of other countries, and the Danish Technological Institute is involved in setting up similar schemes in a number of these.

Alliances across borders

While the Danes promote cooperation between domestic firms, what are the prospects for cross-border alliances? The European Commission has established a directorate (DG 23) devoted to helping Europe's estimated 13.4 million SMEs participate in the Single Market. One initiative is the setting up of European information Centres (EICs or 'Euro-Guichets'), of which there were 191 at the end of 1990. These provide information to SMEs about aspects of Community policy and factors affecting trade within it. Two other initiatives aim to help SMEs network more effectively. The first, BC-NET, is a computerized data base of 14,000 SMEs across Europe that are interested in finding cross-border partners for commercial, technical or financial cooperation. The impact of this, however, has been questionable (Berney, 1990). A subsequent initiative has been a pilot project to encourage groups of twenty to thirty SMEs to commission research from third parties (CRAFT – 'Cooperative Research Action for Technology').

Again, however, we return to the importance of the domestic setting. Pietsch (1991), in research partly undertaken at Warwick Business School, assembles some interesting data which points to the similar conclusion that domestic strengths are critical. Drawing

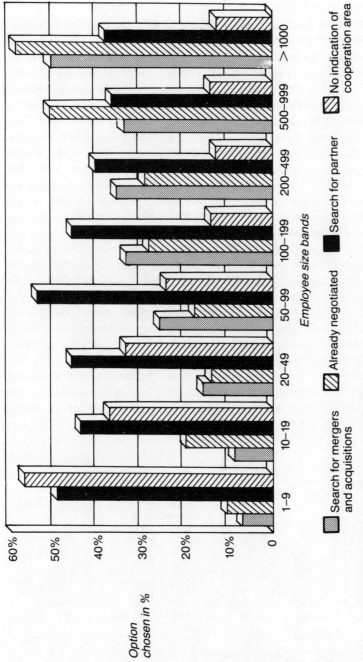

Figure 3.1 Strategic choice: cooperation as a strategic option
Source: Pietsch (1991)

on survey data in 1989 ('Euro-Dialog') for the North Rhine–Westphalia region, Pietsch identifies percentages of firms seeking cooperation partners within the EC (as well as those seeking fully-fledged mergers and acquisitions) according to different size bands. This shows the search for a partner is, first, unexpectedly high, with between 41 per cent and 54 per cent of SMEs within the different bands below 500 employees looking for partners; but, second, that the proportion having formed a cooperative alliance, or having a clear idea of what kind of cooperation would benefit them, or what kind of partner they should look for, is low. The proportions rise with size, and are greatest among firms in the two largest size bands (500–999, and over 1,000 employees). A very similar pattern occurs, as Figure 3.1 shows, in levels of merger and acquisition activity

The explanation for these contrasts can be discerned in figures for exports among firms in the same region provided by the Institut für Mittelstandsforschung (IFM – the institute for SME research), notwithstanding the sample base for the two surveys is different. As Figure 3.2 shows, export ratios rise in very similar fashion with size. In other words, export ratios are strongly correlated with knowing potential partners and with the clinching of partnership agreements.

This is a clear example of the point illustrated in the 'Pressings' case and argued by the Uppsala and network models of internationalization – being present in a market through exporting

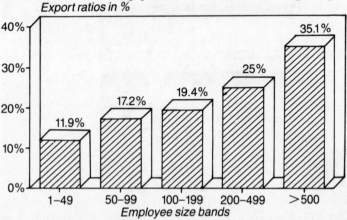

Figure 3.2 Export ratios for enterprises in the manufacturing and mining sector of North Rhine-Westphalia in 1987
Source: Pietsch (1991)

opens up other opportunities. In particular, what exporting does is to begin to establish the personal relationships on which deeper penetration into markets and further internationalization depends (Johanson and Mattsson, 1988; Johanson and Vahlne, 1990). This is borne out by other data from the IFM survey showing the high proportion of cooperations originated by business contacts (71 per cent) and personal contacts (13 per cent). (The use made of exhibition visits (30 per cent) and institutional sources (19 per cent) might suggest it is possible to bypass exporting and business/personal contacts, but we do not know the extent to which these supplement the latter or are incidental to exporting.) As Pietsch (1991: 13) observes, 'This shows again how crucial personal contacts are. The "human factors" like the building up of trust, reliability, sound standing and business usage are given the highest priority by cooperation partners.'

Pietsch makes two other points of note in respect of the 'Euro-Dialog' and IFM survey data. First, small enterprises have a strong interest in marketing/distribution, production, and procurement, whereas medium-sized enterprises are more interested in cooperating in areas such as R&D and finance/acquisitions. This bears out Buckley, Pass and Prescott's (1990a) view about the need to discriminate 'channel management' in the kind of transactions firms enter into. Second, Germany is the leading export nation in the world. We might therefore expect Germany to be very well placed to develop other forms of internationalization – such as transnational alliances – should the need arise.

Governmental agencies may thus help in the formation of networks among indigeneous firms, but cross-border cooperations and alliances are more likely to benefit from an initial presence in a foreign market, arising from export activity. Exports are the initial source for personal relationships on which deeper organizational relationships can be subsequently built. A country with a high export ratio may therefore have an advantage in subsequent phases of internationalization, so that there is no easy substitute for developing exports.

At the same time, it is obvious that without the ability to speak the potential partner's language, personal relationships, on which alliances depend, cannot form. A recent survey indicating that 62 per cent of German people speak English, while only 8 per cent of Britons speak German, shows that Germany has a considerable advantage in this respect also.

The importance of personal relationships in alliances has particular relevance to the family firm, for whom we suggested in Chapter 2 that alliances could be their salvation. Alliances require a motivation to make them work. At first sight, alliances go against the grain of independence which is the rock on which family firms are built. Given the choice of cooperating or dying, however, they have one compelling motivation, which is that entering into cooperative alliances is an alternative to losing independence completely to larger public firms.

A second factor is that family firms are likely to seek other family firms, with whom they feel a kinship and share a certain culture in common (Gallo and Sveen, 1991). As Gallo and Luostarinen (1991) comment, the culture of family businesses in different countries tends to have some common basic assumptions centred on the importance of family. Any basic assumptions like this which coincide make it easier for strategic alliances to succeed.

Third, since successful alliances, and certainly those involving an exchange of equity, often depend on the personal relationships formed at the outset between the leaders of organizations (Harrigan, 1986), the prominence of the family leader in the family firm may mean any such relationship either succeeds or falls at the outset. Responsibility for developing the relationship is unlikely to be delegated – as it may be in the public company where fundamental differences are only exposed when the principals start to make joint decisions, and the alliance then starts to fall apart.

COOPERATION AND STRATEGIC ALLIANCES AMONG LARGE FIRMS

Cooperative strategic alliances are also an attractive option to larger firms that are internationalizing late or as a route into difficult markets. They are seen as a means to short-cut the time it takes to build necessary management systems, acquire market knowledge, and upgrade expertise (Doz, Prahalad and Hamel, 1990). The management of such partnerships, however, is extremely problematic, the more so as the rationale and scope of international alliances has become increasingly complex and acquired underlying competitive motives (Contractor and Lorange, 1988; Root, 1988).

Pucik (1988) provides a good summary of the issues. In the past, alliances were seen as a means to reduce capital investment, lower risk, and gain access to 'closed' markets by linking with an insider. Nowadays, the rationale is much more related to the speed of technological change and growing competitiveness in global markets. Thus, partners increasingly join forces to develop new technologies and/or to take advantage of complementary development skills. On the face of it, the kind of alliances involved may be no different – joint R&D, manufacturing agreements, and joint bidding consortia to achieve economies of scale, and cross-distribution and cross-licensing to improve market position.

However, the underlying context and motives may be fundamentally competitive. Collaboration is a temporary and tactical adjustment to market conditions, but the long-term aim of the partners is to come out on top. The alliance becomes one of 'competitive collaboration' (Doz, Hamel and Prahalad, 1986). This contrasts with the alliances described above between SMEs, which are conceived in the traditional way, as cooperative arrangements to pool complementary strengths and resources.

While long-term win–win outcomes are feasible and desirable in the case of complementary pooling of strengths and assets, they are unlikely to be so in these newer forms of alliance. The reason is that different things are being exchanged, or 'leveraged'. The one leverages resources; the other leverages competencies:

> cross-licensing, technical agreements, joint development programs . . . , and co-production or co-distribution . . . are examples of alliances that focus primarily on resource leverage. The resources contributed to a partnership usually have a specific market value, be it land, equipment, labor, money, or patents. Both the contribution and withdrawal of resources are explicit and thus relatively simple to control.
>
> In contrast, competencies are fundamentally information-based invisible assets (Itami, 1987) that cannot be readily purchased and their market value is difficult to ascertain. Examples are management and organisational skills, knowledge of the market, or technological capability. Invisible assets are embodied in people within the organisation. These assets represent tacit knowledge that is difficult to understand and that can only be appropriated over time, if at all (Teece, 1987).

(Pucik, 1988: 79)

The accumulation of invisible assets of this kind is the foundation for sustainable competitive advantage (Itami, 1987).

There is an important distinction, then, between traditional forms of cooperative alliance between firms in relatively stable competitive relationships, and 'pre-competitive' alliances where what each partner manages to extract from the relationship may have long-term competitive significance. On the one hand, there are the hundreds of joint venture arrangements between the international oil companies (a relatively stable industry at the present time), and those which feature strongly in Morris and Hegert's (1987) study – motor vehicles, aerospace, telecommunications, computers, and other electrical industries, where there is rapid technological change as well as substantial entry costs and risks in rapidly changing markets.

This concern about the nature of alliances has been triggered in the USA by the apparent success of Japanese companies in appropriating and accumulating knowledge through their alliances with Western (American and British) firms, and a number of writers have used such alliances to account for the loss of global market position to Japanese firms (Reich and Mankin, 1986).

Although this argument may be overstated and smack of sour grapes, it does point to an important feature of alliances, as an opportunity for learning. A central issue is who benefits – who learns what from the relationship? The ability to extract more ('asymmetric learning') is attributed to a superior capacity for organizational learning. The Japanese apparently have it because they have 'put in place managerial systems that encourage extensive horizontal and vertical information flow and support the transfer of know-how from the partnership to the rest of the organisation' (Pucik, 1988: 81).

The learning achieved by partners is a critical outcome of any strategic alliance. Such learning therefore cannot be left to chance, but must be part of a systematic and deliberate approach to organizational learning. There must be a clear strategy for the control of invisible assets in a partnership and for learning itself. The policies which guide the management of human resources at all levels and in all functions constitute a vital part of the learning infrastructure which contributes to this.

Table 3.1 Obstacles to organizational learning in international strategic alliances

HR function	Key obstacles
HR planning:	• Strategic intent not communicated • Short-term and static planning horizon • Low priority of learning activities • Lack of involvement by the HR function
Staffing:	• Insufficient lead-time for staffing decisions • Resource-poor staffing strategy • Low quality of staff assigned to the alliance • Staffing dependence on the partner
Training and development	• Lack of cross-cultural competence • Uni-directional training programmes • Career structure not conducive to learning • Poor climate for transfer of learning
Appraisal and rewards	• Appraisal focused on short-term goals • No encouragement of learning • Limited incentives for transfer of know-how • Rewards not tied to global strategy
Organizational design and control	• Responsibility for learning not clear • Fragmentation of the learning process • Control over the HR function given away • No insight into partner's HR strategy

Source: Pucik, V. (1988) 'Obstacles to organisational learning in international strategic alliances', *Human Resource Management* 27(1): 77–93. Copyright © 1988 John Wiley & Sons Inc. Reprinted by permission of John Wiley & Sons Inc.

Learning in alliances

Pucik identifies various ways in which human resource systems fail to provide the basis for effective learning among Western firms in their joint ventures in Japan. Table 3.1 summarizes these. Much of this failure centres on lack of involvement, lack of preparation, and failure to formulate learning as a prime objective.

Hamel (1991) echoes these sentiments and develops some of

the fine detail of what takes place inside partnerships, based on the concerns most often expressed by losers in the relationship. Thus, there is a distinction between internalizing a partner's skills (their core competencies) and just gaining access to some defined area of expertise for a specific purpose. 'Competitive collaboration' should lead one not to expect a partnership to be long-term and indefinite, or entirely harmonious. If this were the case, it might be indicative of a failure of one or both parties to learn. Collaboration should be viewed as a 'race to learn', the alliance as a transitional stage, and the relationship as a bargain which obsolesces.

Western firms in partnerships with Japanese firms expressed concerns of three kinds in Hamel's research – the intent of their partners; how open ('transparent') they were; and their own ability to absorb skills from their partner. Thus, as in Pucik's account, having a deliberate intent to extract lessons from what the partner does is central. This means that employees at large must have a clear view of the partnership as a vehicle for learning. Once it comes to be viewed as simply an alternative to the company doing something for itself – two parties contributing specialized roles – the company is vulnerable to unwittingly giving away key bits of knowledge. Employees must know that they can refuse to talk about certain things.

The corollary to this is being receptive to learning. If a company, and its employees, enters a relationship believing itself to be the senior partner, it is less likely to recognize what it can learn from the other. A readiness to learn is therefore critical. While Western firms are less likely these days to take this view of Japanese partners (although they may be quite capable of having this view of one another), they may, however, come up against another problem which inhibits learning. This hinges on whether the alliance is seen by employees as a proactive step to further expansionary business goals (the perspective of a late-comer), or as an easy way out of a deteriorating competitive situation (the perspective of the laggard). The latter carries with it the stigma of failure and a sense of resignation which is not conducive to learning. By contrast, this does not attach to an alliance to close a specific skills gap.

As a result, the laggard may confront two cruel paradoxes (Hamel, 1991: 97). First, learning often cannot begin until unlearning has taken place – the situation of the failing laggard by definition involves a lot of behaviour which needs replacing.

Second, failure implies a tightening of resources – but to build capability may require an investment in resources. This corresponds to the old truth that a small crisis helps learning, but a large one hinders it.

A third issue concerns the extent of the skills gap. A firm must be able to 'retrace' the steps between its present competence level and that of its partner. If the gap between partners is too great, learning becomes impossible because the laggard cannot identify how the partner got to where it is. A number of writers (for example, Hayes and Wheelwright 1984) have built this insight into learning curve theories of manufacturing to argue that firms must build systematically through a series of clearly defined stages, which they cannot by-pass, in order to reach Japanese standards. However, the ability of Western companies to learn manufacturing competence from the Japanese is impeded, according to Hamel, by the 'inherently lower level of transparency' of production skills, as compared with product designs and market knowledge which in the past Western firms have contributed in such alliances.

A closer look at what transpires in the collaborative relationship, aside of these conditioning factors, shows two related processes standing out. One is the constant pressure of each partner on the other for information, which may or may not be granted. The other is the partners' capacity to process and absorb this:

> knowledge is traded between partners in an on-going process of *collaborative exchange*. As operating employees interact day-by-day, and continually process partner requests for access, a series of micro-bargains are reached . . . . A firm may be in a weak bargaining position at the macro level, . . . but may be able to strike a series of advantageous micro-bargains if, at the operational level, it uniquely possesses the capacity to learn . . . [T]he cumulative impact of micro-bargains will, to a large extent, determine in whose favor future macro-bargains are resolved.
>
> (Hamel, 1991: 101)

Like Pucik, Hamel attributes this ability to learn at the operational level to the qualities of teamwork, at which Japanese firms excel. Teamwork helps to translate individual learning into collective knowledge.

The notion of the collaborative exchange as a series of 'micro-bargains' is important because it emphasizes the informal aspect of a partnership. As Hamel notes, most writers on alliances

(Harrigan, 1988; Killing, 1983; Schillaci, 1987; Tybejee, 1988) have been preoccupied with the formal terms of alliance agreements that define the structures, controls, and allocation of tasks between partners. However, in his own study, Hamel found that

> The greater the experience of interviewees in administering or working within collaborative arrangements, the more likely were they to discount the extent to which the formal agreement actually determined patterns of learning, control, and dependence within their partnerships. The formal agreement was essentially static, and the race for capability acquisition and control essentially dynamic.

(Hamel, 1991: 89)

This view of alliances is echoed characteristically in the view of internationalization as a network of exchange relationships:

> formal cooperation does not often lead to real cooperation, and ... real cooperation is often not visible ... informal cooperation is developed by those who are directly involved in the business exchange between firms, usually line managers on the middle management level. In contrast, formal cooperation between firms is usually entered into on a higher management level with comparatively high involvement of staff [i.e. non-line managers].

(Hakansson and Johanson, reprinted in Ford, 1990: 464)

Similarly, licensing, which is relatively susceptible to tight definition, has been described as 'a relationship rather than an act' (Contractor, 1980: 47). When a firm licences a technology for use by another, it transfers two things: rights to the patentable technology, and non-patentable know-how (Welch, 1985). The latter is generally regarded by users as the more critical part. An important question therefore is how far the licensor is prepared to go in supporting the licensee through a continuing relationship beyond formal documentation. Even licenses, then, which are often regarded as a 'post-competitive' form of alliance that exchanges specified resources, have a certain fluidity which puts a premium on relationships and learning.

Human resource management in alliance relationships

Thus, for whatever kind of alliance we are talking about, involving both large and small firms, the informal aspect of cooperation is of critical importance. Cooperation depends on personal relationships at numerous points between firms. However, personal relationships do not operate in a vacuum. The formal management of human resources determines the basis on which people from one firm interact with those of the other, through the understanding they have of their roles and their motivation.

Multiple relationships at the personal level are of critical importance in forming, sustaining, and learning from alliances. The contribution of formal human resource management to this lies in such things as the selection, preparation, and motivation of individuals who play an active part in the alliance. Teamwork then helps to translate individual learning into collective knowledge.

With this in mind, Lorange (1986) identifies six problem areas for HRM, according to how deep a commitment a multinational alliance involves for the participating organizations (its 'strategic importance') and how much control they seek to exercise. Thus, four kinds of cooperative venture can be distinguished, ranging from temporary project structures to full-blown joint ventures with organization structures that are intended to be permanent. Each of these presents a different slant on the six problem areas, namely:

- who is assigned from each partner – for example, the assignment of 'second-stringers' can create friction;
- who controls those assigned, so that the parent organizations can protect their claim to particular individuals as strategic resources;
- how many staff are assigned, so that the cooperative venture has enough slack to address strategic issues of self-renewal and self-development as well as operational issues;
- how staff, who are assigned to the cooperative venture, are appraised and by whom – performance criteria need to be established at the outset as part of a clear set of objectives for the venture;
- how potential conflicts of loyalty between assigned staff and the parent organization are managed;
- how careers and benefits are protected – including employment rights, the understanding people have about returning to the parent organization, and how helpfully re-entry is managed.

How a firm participating in an alliance manages these issues determines whether the employees it contributes feel they are parties to a divorce from the parent company, or to a marriage with a partner.

A further issue, embracing all these points, is what form the HRM function itself should take. Only in the case of the full joint venture is there likely to be a specialist HRM function independent of the parent organizations. As with other aspects of the whole relationship, issues of compatibility between HRM functions, in terms of culture and style, may have to be addressed. These will soon make themselves felt if there exist any fundamental differences in philosophy underlying the systems of pay and benefits, appraisal, selection, and promotion that are being matched up within the cooperative venture. In the case of the fully-fledged joint venture, this will become a third party, with perhaps a third different way of doing things.

In addition to the interpersonal aspects of cooperation, then, there are important issues of control and strategic flexibility which underly the success of transnational collaboration (Doz, Prahalad and Hamel, 1990). This parallels one of the core issues in how multinationals manage employees in subsidiaries – namely, the degree of control exercised from the centre. This is the starting point for most analyses of HRM in internationalized firms, to which we turn in the next chapter.

CONCLUSION

The international economy is increasingly characterized by diverse, complex, multiple network relationships. Far from being a step between export and foreign direct investment, large multinationals increasingly make use of alliances as an extension of their international operations. Alliances are not an alternative, but add to the range of their international strategies. Thus, Dicken (1992: 213) comments that 'although strategic alliances are not confined to particular sizes or types of firm, they are undoubtedly more common between large TNCs [transnational companies] with extensive international operations'. Moreover:

> According to a Business International (1987: 113–114) study, relationships are increasingly polygamous rather than monogamous: 'Few companies have only a single alliance. Instead, they form a series of alliances, each with partners that

have their own web of collaborative arrangements. Companies like Toshiba, Philips, AT&T and Olivetti are at the hub of what are often overlapping alliance networks which frequently include a number of fierce competitors.' As a result it becomes more and more difficult to establish the precise boundaries between firms.

(Dicken, 1992: 213)

In this chapter, we have considered alliances between SMEs as a defensive manoeuvre against take-over or domination by larger firms. If we were to take account, however, of the extent of subcontracting relationships in which SMEs are embedded and to which they often owe their livelihood, we would find large, international firms very much in evidence. As Dicken (1992: 226) says, 'The TNC not only directly controls and co-ordinates its own complex internal networks at an international or global scale but also indirectly controls many of the external networks in which it is embedded.' As a result, any one organization's strength in this system does not depend simply on the specific advantages it may have, 'but more upon its network linkages' (McKiernan, 1992: 108). However comprehensive in other respects, Dunning's (1988) 'eclectic paradigm' of the internationalization process seems not to fully embrace this possibility.

Networking among firms, whichever way we look at it, is a ubiquitous phenomenon in the modern international economy. In Chapter 2, we described the process of forming networks. In this chapter, having considered the motives for entering alliances, we have focused more particularly on operating within networks. This emphasizes the importance of learning; how this takes place through detailed patterns of information exchange; and how individual knowledge and information is translated into organizational learning through participation in teams.

The analysis of learning in alliances is relatively new, however, and the notion of information exchange is misleading. Although Hamel's 'core competences' approach supposedly treats the process as more than a gaining of access to a defined area of expertise, the tendency is still to treat the learning goal as the 'internalisation of a partner's skills and capabilities' (Inkpen, 1991). However, managers are often surprised to find that the secret of Japanese success lies not in any sophisticated technology differences, but in the simplicity of things and an attitude of seeking continuous improvement for improvement's sake. As one of the American managers Inkpen interviewed commented:

> Most Western companies enter a joint venture expecting to find visible differences that are not only unique but unknown to the rest of industry. The reality is that the differences will be unique but they will be subtle. The differences require an understanding of the Japanese approach to business and the importance they place on the soft side. In most cases, the differences are going to be managerial rather than technological – a recognition that there are important differences requires an admission that American managerial practice may be part of the problem. Many managers find that hard to admit.
>
> (Inkpen, 1991: 16)

Part of the learning problem, then, is what an alliance partner expects to learn. It then highlights change in management attitudes (a key human resource variable) as a key focus for learning. This was especially apparent in the case of joint ventures in Inkpen's study, where American managers began to doubt there was learning to be achieved, simply because they began to judge a joint venture a failure because it was not meeting their (un-Japanese) expectations of profitability in the early stages. The idea of 'core competences', if it is to be of use in understanding organizational learning, has therefore to accommodate managerial attitudes rooted in the national culture.

Chapter 4

Human resource management in the international firm

THE NATURE AND IMPORTANCE OF INTERNATIONAL FIRMS

The central theme of Dicken's (1992) recent book, *Global Shift: The Internationalization of Economic Activity*, is that transnational corporations (TNCs) are the single most important force in the modern world economy. For example, it is estimated that between one-fifth and one-quarter of total world production in the world's market economies is performed by transnationals, dominated by a core group of 600 such firms (UNCTC, 1988). Among these, just seventy-four firms account for half of all sales, or 10 per cent of total world production. An increasing proportion of the resulting trade, moreover, is carried out between units of these TNCs – that is, inside the TNCs. In the United States and Japan more than 50 per cent of total trade (exports and imports) is carried out within TNCs, and possibly as much as 80 per cent of the UK's manufactured exports are from either UK-owned or UK-based foreign multinationals (Dicken, 1992: 49).

International companies are therefore of increasing importance to international trade, while economic activity in the developed countries is increasingly concentrated in relatively few large organizations. As Bartlett and Ghoshal (1989: 115) comment, 'trade is increasingly carried out among the various units of individual MNCs [multinational corporations], as companies import goods manufactured in their off-shore plants or export products to be sold by wholly-owned foreign subsidiaries'. A European Commission report similarly observes:

> The exchange of goods and services on an arm's-length and *ad hoc* basis, i.e. 'trade' in a textbook sense, between independent

firms in two countries, is becoming the exception rather than the rule. Contractual relationships between links in the 'chain of value added' are becoming an essential feature of the modern economy.

(Commission of the European Communities, 1988a)

There is one other factor which distinguishes the large international firm, and that is the fact that innovation and the ability to harness it inside the organization is a key source of competitive advantage in the modern world economy:

A firm invests abroad to derive further profit from innovations developed for the domestic market. Its market entrée in many countries is its ability to innovate (i.e. to develop new products and processes) and to create an organisation through which it can appropriate the benefits of its innovations more advantageously than by selling or licensing its technology.

In the current international environment, a company's ability to innovate rapidly is becoming *the* primary source of competitive advantage.

(Bartlett and Ghoshal, 1989: 115)

Bartlett and Ghoshal thus point to the ability to innovate and the ability to transfer these innovations between units of the large firm around the world. The transnational goes beyond both 'central innovation processes' and 'local innovation processes' which characterize what they call respectively the 'global firm' and the 'multinational corporation'. The true 'transnational', by virtue of its flexibility, is able to connect resources, innovations, and entrepreneurship which are spread throughout the company.

This need for flexibility, their size, complexity, and the fact that they operate across national borders, create problems for the management of human resources. To have a proper grasp of the HRM issues, though, we need to be clearer about the kind of organization we are talking about. As Dicken rightly comments, transnationals take a multitude of forms and vary greatly in size, with the majority having a relatively limited geographical spread. Bartlett and Ghoshal are clearly using the term 'transnational' in a more specific way than Dicken (and others) use it, and we need therefore to clarify terms. The next section does so by outlining a model for the evolution of the strategies and structures of international firms. This provides the background to the patterns of staffing in international firms and the shifts in HRM activity which occur as they change and grow.

Forms of international organization

Interest in the structures of international companies is part of a longstanding concern within strategic management with requisite forms of organization to implement strategy effectively (the 'structural fit' hypothesis). Its pedigree includes the work of Chandler (1962), Scott (1971), Channon (1973), Stopford and Wells (1972), Salter (1973), and Rumelt (1974). Much of this work has tended towards the explication of stages in the development of organizational forms, as firms elaborate their involvement in new products and new geographical areas.

Within international management, the work of Stopford and Wells (1972) is seminal, since it was among the first specifically to focus on the development of the international company. Their study of 187 large US-based companies operating world-wide and the stages model they proposed has become, as Bartlett and Ghoshal (1989: 30) note, 'the benchmark for much subsequent research, consulting advice, and practice'. Using the variables of the number of products sold internationally ('foreign product diversity') and the importance of international sales to the company ('foreign sales as a percentage of total sales'), they suggested that international firms follow a pattern of development more or less as follows:

A

foreign sales/product diversity → international division
(low)   (low)

Bi

foreign sales/product diversity → area division
(high)   (low)

or

Bii

foreign sales/product diversity → world-wide product
(low)   (high)   division

C

foreign sales/product diversity → global matrix (or 'grid')
(high)   (high)

As Bartlett and Ghoshal (1989: 31) observe, however:

the [resulting] debate was often reduced to simplistic choices between 'centralisation' and 'decentralisation', or to generalised discussions of the comparative value of product- and geography-based structures.

(Bartlett and Ghoshal, 1989: 31)

As an organizational panacea for coping with increasing complexity, diversity, and change in the 1980s, moreover, the global matrix proved to be 'an organisational quagmire' (Bartlett and Ghoshal 1989:31) from which international firms were forced to retreat.

Most recent work has been concerned with modelling new forms of organization which take account of the true extent of complexity and the needs for internal coordination. Coupled with this, there is a growing body of literature on the concept of competitive advantage, the nature of international markets, and international competitive strategies, deriving from Porter (1986), which provides the backdrop to forms of organization. The evolution of these concepts and of firms' strategies can be seen in successive characterizations of the international firm since the early 1970s – from the multinational corporation (1960s/70s), via the global firm (1980s) and international company (1980s/90s), to the present-day transnational (1990s) – although predating any of these by centuries are the trading companies and international holding companies which followed the spread of European empires around the world.

The modern, complex international firm first manifested itself as the 'multinational corporation' (MNC). This came to be defined as an organization having production assets in at least six countries and at least 25 per cent of its profits and £100 million of sales abroad. The MNC secured competitive advantage by being able to mobilize resources, primarily capital and cash, to extend its operations into new territories. In other ways, however, it was a loose association of independent operating units:

[The MNC is] essentially a decentralised federation; overseas operations are regarded as a portfolio of largely independent, nationally oriented businesses. The competitive advantages enjoyed by such a firm are primarily specific to a country.

(Spivey and Thomas, 1990)

When it was first identified, the MNC often attracted opprobrium as a vehicle of cultural uniformity and dollar imperialism (Vernon, 1971, 1977). In reality, most such firms pursued strategies that were essentially 'multi-domestic', being oriented to national markets with relatively low organizational integration. Since Porter, such a collection of nationally oriented businesses is, therefore, now often referred to as a 'multidomestic' firm.

In the early 1980s, Levitt (1983) described the conditions for the 'global firm'. He argued that markets were tending towards increased 'globalization'. They were becoming more like one another – more 'homogenized' – as people of different countries developed similar consumer tastes and demands. For the international firm this implied more standardized products; uniform approaches to marketing; locating plant and other activities in advantageous places around the globe, according to local advantages such as low costs, skilled labour, or the availability of scientists; and integrating competitive strategies across countries (Yip, 1989). This kind of firm implies a high degree of integration managed from a corporate centre. In this way, it can extract economies of scale and scope from world-wide activities and exploit national factor differences (Porter, 1985; Ghoshal, 1987). It supposedly operates 'with few, if any, self-imposed geographic or organisational constraints on where or how it conducts its business operations' (Reilly and Campbell, 1990: 63).

In practice, a number of firms which in the past were called MNCs already operated in this way on global (or at least regional) market principles. Ford of Europe, for example, typified this kind of operation, with its attempt to exploit advantages of scale in R&D and purchasing, and the switching of manufacture between countries according to cost and delivery criteria.

More recently, there has been a retreat from some of the simplifications of globalism which assume that competitive advantage comes from standardization, large scale, and low cost alone. Instead, there is said to be a trend for firms to have to meet distinctive needs in different markets (Hamel and Prahalad, 1989). For example, washing machines in Europe run at different temperatures and speeds because Italians, French, British and Germans differ in their views about what is best for washing clothes. As a result, a product like washing powder, which is often used as the symbol of a uniform product, has to be adapted to different washing conditions. A more extreme example, the European pharmaceuticals industry, is notoriously fragmented, with the French, for example, preferring to take their potions as suppositories while the British take theirs orally. Tendencies towards different ailments also differ. In addition, greater affluence encourages people to move away from standardized products to want more variable consumer goods and more frequent changes in these. Developments in flexible manufacturing also make this more feasible (Bartlett and Yosihara, 1988).

These considerations require firms to be flexible. The international company gains its advantage from being able to apply its knowledge and skills world-wide to local circumstances – or as the jargon puts it, being able to 'leverage' its core competencies into national markets. This is in addition, of course, to its ability to 'leverage' material resources, such as cash, into different markets. What it is doing, then, is mobilizing its people resources of skill and knowledge on an international scale. This kind of organization, which Bartlett and Ghoshal (1989) simply call the 'international company', requires relative centralization through its planning systems and leadership, somewhere between that of the MNC and global firm. However, the style of centralization is a lot more sophisticated and involves much more complex problems in the management of people.

Bartlett and Ghoshal (1989), and Bartlett, Doz, and Hedlund (1990) have characterized one more type of international firm, which they call the 'transnational organization'. This supposedly is an organization which can simultaneously respond to the forces of global integration, local differentiation, *plus* world-wide innovation in technologies and products. This captures, then, their contention that innovation and the ability to harness it is the key source of competitive advantage in the modern world. Mobilizing skills and knowledge is not just about communicating market knowledge. It also means transferring innovations from the centre to local markets, and from local centres to the centre and other localities. The transnational aims to connect resources, innovations, and entrepreneurship which are spread throughout the company.

Bartlett and Ghoshal argue that this means developing simultaneously the characteristics associated with the MNC, the global firm, and the international company – that is, responsiveness to local conditions, efficiency, and the ability to handle continuous innovation and learning. Competitive advantage will come from sensing needs in one market, responding with capabilities perhaps developed in a second, and diffusing any resulting innovations to markets and facilities around the globe (Bartlett and Ghoshal, 1989: 12).

These changes in the character of the international firm over the last twenty to thirty years are summarized in Table 4.1.

Although new organizational forms have evolved as the international economy has become more complex and new opportunities have emerged, this is not to say by any means that such shifts have been widespread or uniform (although some writers may well give that impression). All types of organization coexist within and across sectors, depending on the characteristics of different sectors, firms' strategies, and where they are starting from. Different types of firm are suited to the demands of different sectors, according to how fragmented or cohesive markets themselves are and the transferability of technologies and processes.

Managing complexity, including the movement of people, nevertheless, is a common and growing phenomenon. This presents, above all, a challenge to management thinking. Indeed, Bartlett and Ghoshal (1989:17) argue that the transnational is not a particular organizational form so much as a new management mentality. It implies a high degree of flexibility and diversity in organization structures and systems, and in management psychology, education, and working practices. Even if the transnational form is an unattainable ideal – and Bartlett and Ghoshal acknowledge that examples are hard to find – flexibility is a key management quality in many types of international firm, including those in their study which they define as 'international companies' (viz. General Electric, Proctor and Gamble, and Ericsson). As they observe, 'Most managers seemed to understand very clearly the nature of the *strategic task* they faced; their main problem was developing and managing the *organisational capability* to implement the new and more complex global strategies' (Bartlett and Ghoshal, 1989: x).

A note on internalization and externalization

The definition of the transnational which Dicken adopts, stressing coordination across national boundaries, although looser, recognizes the same phenomenon. Where there is a difference, however, is in the greater emphasis on external collaboration, and

Table 4.1 Strategy, structure, knowledge and skills in the international firm

	MNC	Global firm	International company	Transnational
Strategic focus	Exploit local national opportunities; mobilize capital and cash into additional countries. (multidomestic)	Standardize products in homogenized world markets; integrate and coordinate country strategies; exploit low cost locations for production, and high skill locations for R&D.	Meet local tastes for differentiated products (through adaptation of basic lines?).	Locally responsive; globally efficient; continuously innovative.
Organization	Decentralized; low integration.	High integration; managed from corporate centre.	Flexible centralization.	Coordination of interdependent units, nationally and world-wide; high flexibility, diversity, complexity.
Knowledge and skills	Country-specific knowledge and skills, retained locally.	Global standardization; global economies and centralized knowledge of R&D, production, purchasing, marketing.	Leverage central core competencies into national markets.	Develop, transfer and diffuse specialized knowledge and skills from wherever found to wherever required.

Source: Adapted from Bartlett and Ghoshal (1989: 65)

the multiple forms that takes (see Chapter 3). Dicken, like the network theorists, is more explicit about the interplay of external and internal networks, whereas Bartlett and Ghoshal give the impression that the flexibility they talk about is all contained within the transnational corporation. In network terms, large international firms need to be able to mobilize, within their internal structures, knowledge and other resources accumulated in a variety of both internal and external networks, in order to apply these to new markets and gain better synergies in existing ones.

Nevertheless, the work of Bartlett and Ghoshal has provided a focus for a stream of work concerned with innovatory and looser organization structures. Several essays in Bartlett, Doz and Hedlund (1990) describe similar organizational forms which capture this internal–external fluidity – Hedlund and Rolander with their 'heterarchy'; Kogut with his 'global network'; and White and Poynter with their 'horizontal organisation'. Kanter (1989) similarly argues that competitive advantage will be based on flatter organization structures which can mobilize entrepreneurial activity more effectively within the firm, while handling strategic alliances without. In these ways, these authors are moving beyond the conventional idea of a 'strategy–structure fit' to a broader notion of 'organisational capability'.

However, much of this writing is normative, rather than being a rigorous test of empirical differences which define superior performance in relation to levels of internationalization or differences in organizational form. One study which attempted this found that organizational factors explained twice as much variance in profit as economic factors (Geringer, Beamish and daCosta, 1989). Such findings are important, but rare. The implication is that special attention should be directed towards processes within firms, such as HRM, and the forms of organization people operate within.

The descriptions above of the development of the international firm consistently emphasize three factors, or sets of advantage, which the international firm enjoys or seeks to capitalize on – 'ownership-specific advantages' (the competitive advantage which is the well-spring for its move abroad), 'locational advantages' (the benefit of conducting some aspect of its activities in one place rather than another because of factor costs), and 'internalization advantages' (the advantages of doing something inside the firm rather than leasing, selling, or leaving it to another). Dunning (1988) has combined these in his 'eclectic paradigm' of internationalization.

Bartlett and Ghoshal's (1989) 'ideal' organizational type, the transnational, echoes Dunning's argument that leveraging transaction cost advantages (or 'internalization') is the key factor in the growth of the international firm in the long-term. In principle, however, transaction cost minimization simply determines the degree to which a firm gathers into itself all those activities which could alternatively be carried out through market mechanisms (Buckley and Casson, 1976; Rugman, 1981; Buckley, 1983, 1988; Casson, 1987). Where transaction costs favour the firm, the firm grows and extends itself into progressively more national markets and into more aspects of those markets through a process of 'internalization'. The implication in Bartlett and Ghoshal is that international firms are heading increasingly in this direction. The theory of transaction costs suggests, however, that there are potential limits to the growth of the firm *vis-à-vis* its markets. It therefore serves as an antidote to bland assumptions about the inexorable growth of the 'global firm'.

In summary, the theory of transaction costs and internalization gives theoretical underpinning to recent developments in organizational form described in the business strategy literature, while pointing to the variety of forms which exist and the degree of externalized activity which occurs. Inside the international firm, the theory sets parameters for viewing centralization versus decentralization tendencies, while many issues for the management of human resources rest, in turn, on the degree of centralization or decentralization through the effect this has on internal labour markets.

STRUCTURAL CHANGE AND STAFFING IN THE INTERNATIONAL FIRM

Alternative structures and observed trends in organizing for international business provide the starting point for most accounts of human resource issues (for example, Atkinson, 1989; Evans, Doz and Laurent, 1989; Dowling and Schuler, 1990; Bartlett, Doz and Hedlund, 1990; Barham and Oates, 1991). At the heart of this is the tension between centralization and decentralization in managing organizations, with international firms increasingly seeking to combine the benefits of both centralization and decentralization.

The four types of international organization in Table 4.1 imply different patterns of control and consequently different sets of practices for moving staff about the organization. Some years ago, before these types of organization had themselves emerged, Perlmutter (1969) defined the choices in terms of ethnocentric polycentric, regiocentric, and geocentric staffing. These differ as follows:

1 *Ethnocentric staffing:* Strategic decisions are made at headquarters, subsidiaries have limited autonomy, and key jobs at home and abroad are filled by employees from headquarters. Nationals from the parent country rule the organization both at home and (as expatriates) abroad.

2 *Polycentric staffing:* Each subsidiary is treated as a distinct national entity with local control of operations, but the head-quarters controls key financial targets and investment decisions. Subsidiaries are managed by local nationals, but the key headquarters jobs remain with staff from the parent country.

3 *Regiocentric staffing:* Control within the group and the movement of staff is managed on a regional basis, reflecting the particular disposition of businesses and operations within the group. Regional managers have greater discretion in decisions. But movement of staff is largely restricted to geographic regions, and promotion to the very top jobs continues to be dominated by managers from the parent country.

4 *Geocentric staffing:* Business strategy is integrated on a thoroughly global basis. Staff development and promotion is based on ability, rather than nationality. The board and other parts of the top management structure are thoroughly international in composition.

Almost everything else in international HRM flows from the way the firm manages its movement of staff in one or other of these ways. Thus, the overall approach to staffing determines the degree of attention given, and the opportunities available, to each of three groups of employee – parent-country nationals (PCNs), host-country nationals (HCNs), and third-country nationals (TCNs) (Dowling and Schuler, 1990). PCNs come from the country where the firm has its corporate headquarters; HCNs are nationals of a country where a subsidiary is located and for which they work; and

TCNs are from outside both. For instance, a German manager taking up a position in a French subsidiary of a UK-based firm would be a TCN.

As staffing policy shifts, so too does the attention given to different kinds of HRM activity. As a firm becomes progressively more internationalized, attention is likely to shift from the selection of expatriates (PCNs) and the management of their terms and conditions, to training a much larger population (PCNs, HCNs and TCNs) in preparation for shorter, more frequent assignments, and managing their development through a formal career system. Eventually, one is likely to see a broader educational effort to internationalize the organization at large – that is, a focus on cultural change. This will include influencing the attitudes and perspectives of employees who are not likely to go abroad, but who need to have an international outlook on the total business.

Although these shifts are driven by the product-markets and industries the firm is in, it is important to note the role played also by the socio-cultural environments in which the international firm operates (Evans and Lorange, 1989). For instance, Dowling and Schuler observe that:

> US MNCs [multinationals companies] are increasing their use of TCNs and HCNs mainly for cost and political reasons. As they do, the issues of training and retaining TCNs and HCNs will grow in importance and MNCs will have to give more consideration to career opportunities and career paths for TCNs and HCNs.
>
> (Dowling and Schuler, 1990: 70)

Equally, a normally regiocentric or geocentric organization may adopt an ethnocentric approach on occasion if, for example, it establishes itself in a new country that, for the moment, does not have appropriate skills. More generally, regional units may take on an ethnocentric stance within their own territory.

For reasons such as these, the ethnocentric, polycentric, regiocentric, and geocentric patterns of staffing do not correspond precisely to the four types of firm (MNC, global, international company and transnational).

BP: A case study of shifts in strategy, structure, staffing and HRM

A good example of shifts in structure and staffing policy is provided by BP, the UK's largest company in terms of sales. BP has changed its structure over the years to manage an increasing complexity of operations and a changing portfolio of products and markets. In the process, it has developed different ways of managing its international employees. The example below, drawn from interviews in the company during 1991, traces the impact of strategy and structure on BP's staffing practices.

The background to BP's evolution is the fact that the oil industry needed to be international to bring sources of oil from various parts of the world to consumer markets elsewhere. Having found large reserves of oil, they then needed to open up suitable consumer markets. The five or six major companies that made the market for oil were therefore integrated to varying degrees. Some, like BP and Exxon, tended towards a high degree of centralization and integration. Others, like Shell (formed from a Dutch company that found oil and a British trading company) managed the relationship between exploration/production and refining/distribution through arm's-length companies. Thus, Shell had a more decentralist character from the outset. (Since the world market for oil was formed, there are, in fact, other companies that do operate just as production *or* distribution companies.)

From the beginning, each company tended to have a particular sphere of influence. BP's was initially Iran (at that time known as Persia), from where it developed production sources across the Middle East during the 1950s and 1960s. This was still the case at the time of the Yom Kippur war in 1973, between Israel and the Arab countries. For the oil industry, the major consequence of the 1973 war was OPEC's use of its cartel to force up oil prices, in order to put economic pressure on the West, and thereby on Israel. The effect on companies like BP was to generate an enormous increase in revenue. Subsequently, BP also developed additional major new reserves in Alaska and the North Sea. The effect of these two together was that BP found itself with a growing cash mountain.

These windfall riches generated a period of diversification through acquisition. This included ventures into chemicals, animal feeds and other businesses like coal which it has since got out of. These markets themselves exhibited varying degrees of internationalization, but generally were far less international than oil.

In the 1980s, expansion then became more focused on the core oil business – first, with the acquisition of Standard Oil of Ohio to give BP the marketing presence it lacked in North America and to provide outlets for its Alaskan oilfield; and, second, with the acquisition of Britoil in the UK, which expanded its production resources.

This series of shifts in the business were accompanied by changes in organization structure and in mind-set about what kind of company BP was:

1   *The 'integrated phase' (1940–70)*: During this period, BP opened up plants throughout the Middle East, and developed markets in Europe, South America, Australasia and the Far East. It was a phase characterized by strong central control and integration, in which overseas businesses were managed as if they were part of domestic operations. As a BP manager put it, 'we would put down a plant in the Middle East and manage it as if it was in South Wales.'

2   *The 'conglomerate phase' (1970s)*: As BP began to put its cash-flows to use through acquisitions, the centre took on the role of banker. New businesses in unfamiliar areas were managed at arm's-length: the incumbent management continued to run operations, while BP exercised control over finance and capital investment.

3   *The 'centralized phase' (1980s)*: The acquisitions of Standard Oil and Britoil, unlike earlier acquisitions, substantially increased the numbers of employees in BP, adding around a third to existing numbers in each case. Moreover, they related directly to the existing core oil business, bringing in comparable skills, and in some cases superior expertise. The initial emphasis therefore was on integrating these businesses and their employees into BP by spreading BP's systems and culture outwards.

4   *The 'horizontal phase' (1990s)*: Standard Oil and Britoil had been sizeable companies, with their distinctive cultures and areas of expertise. Standard Oil, for example, complemented BP's historical strength in oil exploration with marketing expertise,

in which BP had been relatively weak. The latest phase is an acknowledgement of these differences within the group, and a recognition that 'the Brits do not have all the answers'.

The non-oil businesses, moreover, have continued to grow and to pursue their own internationalization strategies. Increasingly, therefore, they have presented alternative centres of power within the group – for instance, animal feeds (Nutrition) has remained headquartered in Holland. BP has been trying to transform itself, therefore, into the kind of 'transnational' described earlier, with multiple centres of power and expertise, which it seeks to leverage into different parts of the whole group.

These shifts in structure and organizational philosophy are neatly summarized in the series of diagrams shown in Figure 4.1, which a BP manager wrote down to describe the company's development. These shifts in organizational structure and control at BP over the years created different human resource requirements, and led to people being moved about the organization in different ways.

In the first phase, to manage overseas plants, the need was to transfer job skills from the UK to countries without such skills. Operations staff of all kinds (plant managers, craftsmen, engineers, plant operators) therefore went abroad on permanent long-term assignments. Typically these were experienced staff, and their assignments lasted around twenty years, until the end of their working lives. The result was a relatively stable population of expatriate Britons, varying from around 1,000 in the late 1950s and rising to a peak of around 1,400. The second phase did not materially change this pattern.

During the third phase, however, while still transferring job skills and maintaining an expatriate workforce in the Middle East, much greater use began to be made of secondments from the UK to newly-acquired overseas companies. A more varied population, including senior managers, marketing and IT staff, went out on shorter assignments (of two to three years), to other areas within their own business and functions. In going abroad, they spread the British company culture; when they returned, the experience they had gained of the foreign operations enabled them to exercise control more effectively from headquarters in London. Thus, out of some 1,500 expatriates in the 1980s, 1,200 were likely to be British, while 300 of these were likely to be on short assignments to the USA where Standard Oil had been acquired.

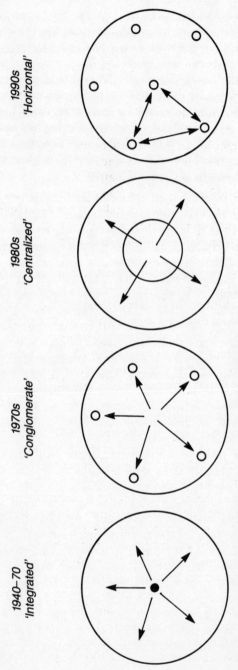

Figure 4.1 Shifts in organizational structure and philosophy in BP

The most recent phase has seen considerable growth in two-way secondments. Many more senior non-British managers are coming to the UK on two- to three-year assignments and going to other parts of the group in order to transfer learning and develop teamwork. The composition of the expatriate population has become much more fluid, less exclusively British (comprising perhaps 1,000 out of 1,500), and less focused on any one geographical area – reflecting the broader spread of assets.

These changes in the nature, extent, duration and direction of assignments at BP have shifted the focus of human resource activity. In the earlier phases, most attention went on transferring terms and conditions to make long-term moves attractive to individuals, and then, organizationally, to bind certain of the new acquisitions (such as coal) into the BP system. In doing so, the personnel function acted as central arbiter, handing down standard conditions.

One- and two-way assignments, however, mean accommodating the interests and development needs of individuals, businesses, and functions, and entail a complex negotiating process between these, rather than direction by a central personnel function. This requires a sophisticated career management system, especially in such a large organization. In practice, in BP, these negotiations are managed through the regional structures of the separate businesses and of the group as a whole. It is often more economic, in fact, for a large company to manage staffing at a regional level, rather than at a completely global level, and BP as a whole is probably part-way between the regiocentric and geocentric models.

However, while the flow of assignments provides the basis for transferring learning and best practice throughout the organization, the key to making this effective is seen as the management of culture, and specifically the creation of a team culture. BP has determined that the way to transfer learning is to build the professional skills of groups, so that not only are the individual skills of the assignee enhanced through developmental assignments, but the host organization learns too.

The creation of a such a culture is an educational process. Considerable effort has therefore gone into developing a new set of cultural values that emphasize teamwork, openness, networking, less fixation on a person's status and more on what they can personally contribute. This has included educational programmes to raise awareness of different cultures within the group (as distinct from cultural training simply to prepare people for assignments abroad, which BP has done for some time).

Backing up direct education, teamworking is being reinforced through a new reward structure (although this is difficult to devise in a management system), and by a new appraisal system. The role and structure of job evaluation has similarly been reviewed. Most head office staff have moved out of the old headquarters with its imperial-colonial ambience; the numbers of permanent head office staff have been reduced; and head office managers now work in open-plan offices. All of these contribute symbolically to the image of a new international-minded company. As one manager put it, 'It feels like a new company.'

Other initiatives, such as the use of non-British centres such as Harvard and INSEAD for top management education, also help to give the group an international character, although they are not part of the process of creating a team culture as such.

The emphasis on team culture, in fact, has two aspects. First, is the reliance on a common groupwide culture to bind the group together and get everyone 'facing the same way'. The other is the specific character of a team culture in minimizing barriers within a large organization.

Other companies, like Shell, give similar emphasis to the need for 'organizational glue' to bind the organization together and make a large international company viable. For Shell, one of the most thoroughly internationalized companies in the world, this 'glue' consists in strongly communicated behavioural values, a written set of ethical business principles (since 1984), socialization through a well-understood reward and promotion structure, a world-wide expatriate cadre of 5,000 managers deployed as a corporate resource, and English as the common language of the group. Since Shell is partly Dutch, the decision on language is all the more significant.

The example of BP outlines many of the general themes and issues in managing firms at different stages of their international development. Table 4.2 summarizes this series of shifts in staffing policy and the focus of HRM, against the background of structural change. The most recent period shows a highly internationalized firm trying to go beyond structure to enforce coordination, to develop what Bartlett and Ghoshal (1989: 174) call a new management mentality – a 'matrix in managers' minds' – rather than relying on a structural matrix. At this point, BP seemed to be hovering between a regiocentric and geocentric posture, to use Perlmutter's terms.

Table 4.2 Shifts in structure, staffing and HRM at BP

Era	Structure	Staffing philosophy	HR objective	Focus of activity
1940–70	integrated	ethnocentric	transfer job-skills	transfer terms and conditions
1970s	conglomerate	polycentric	"	"
1980s	centralized	ethnocentric	create common British company culture by seconding from the UK	career management
1990s	horizontal	regiocentric/ geocentric	transfer learning through two-way secondments and international teams	career management and team culture creation

During 1992, however, BP underwent sudden, further change, with the replacement in June of its chairman and chief executive, Robert Horton, bringing into the open its deteriorating financial situation and uneasy personal relationships within the senior management stemming from Horton's forceful management style. In essence, BP had become over-indebted through its acquisition of Britoil and the purchase of the outstanding 45 per cent of Standard Oil in 1987/88, compounded then by having to buy back, in 1989, £2.5 billion of shares to reduce the holding which the Kuwait Investment Office had built up at the time of BP's privatization. These financial pressures in turn have put the spotlight on the loss-making chemicals business and on the nutritions business which has consistently failed to produce the expected return on capital.

The result is likely to be retrenchment, disposals of non-oil businesses and tighter central controls. In any case, Horton had already put into motion substantial cost-cutting measures, with numbers of staff leaving, while presenting to the world the face of a team-based culture change. These reversals show therefore how superficial evolutionary models of company development can be. A company can move forward along the paths suggested by Bartlett and Ghoshal and Perlmutter, and then backwards again.

HUMAN RESOURCE STRATEGIES IN THE INTERNATIONAL FIRM

The example of BP illuminates many of the general themes and issues for managing the highly internationalized firm. We now turn to a more detailed discussion of these.

We suggested that as a firm becomes progressively more internationalized, attention in HRM can be expected to shift:

1 from the selection of expatriates and the management of their terms and conditions;
2 to training in preparation for assignments and their management through a formal career system with personal development in mind, including the extension of this system to an increasingly diverse and dispersed population;
3 to, eventually, a broader educational effort to internationalize the organization at large.

The following sections deal with these themes in turn to reflect the shifts in focus.

However, as new issues arise, those at an earlier level are never left behind. Instead, they deepen the scale of involvement of the human resources function in internationalization. Dowling (1988) summarizes this increasing involvement, in broad terms, as follows:

• additional functions and activities (international taxation, relocation and orientation, administrative services for expatriates, host government relations, and language services);
• the need for a broader perspective (an awareness of the complex equity issues that arise, for example, when employees of different nationalities work together);

- the greater involvement in employees' lives (more direct contact with the employee's family);
- changing the emphasis of activity as the balance of the workforce between PCNs and HCNs varies;
- exposure to greater risk through the costs of overseas assignments and the high risk of failure; and
- more external influences (through types of government, economies, and ways of doing business).

This deepening involvement impacts directly on the work of the HRM function. The following section focuses therefore on the kind of issues which have tended to dominate discussions of international HRM. While this identifies many qualitative differences between HRM in the domestic and international settings, there are also important continuities which can be exploited in solving some of the most troublesome human resource problems.

The selection and management of expatriates

The use of expatriates represents a transfer of expertise to locations abroad. More especially, though, it is a means of exercising strategic control. A third reason is for management development purposes. Partly, this is to broaden key employees' experience and transfer expertise back to the home country; partly it is to develop a cadre of senior managers for the future with sufficient grasp of the whole organization to be able to run it effectively. As the BP example showed, organizations make use of expatriates in these three ways to different degrees at different stages of internationalization.

In recent years there has been a growing appreciation of the role of expatriates for purposes of strategic control (Torbiorn, 1982; Brewster, 1991). One of the factors in this is apparent cultural differences in the way strategic control is exercised. Bartlett and Ghoshal (1989) distinguish three patterns in their study of nine transnationals. The characteristic Japanese approach ('centralization') depends heavily on the transfer of employees from Japan. The American approach ('formalization'), by contrast, relies on formal systems, policies and standards, through, for example, the imposition of organization-wide strategic planning processes. The European approach ('socialization'), like that of the Japanese, is also people-based, but does not depend to anything like the same degree on the transfer of acolytes from head office. Instead, it uses careful recruitment, development, and acculturation of key decision makers to establish shared values and objectives across diverse nationalities.

These contrasting patterns require deeper investigation, especially since the European model covers many countries. To do this, it would be necessary to have comparative data on the numbers of expatriates and the kind of assignments involved (including duration) among comparable firms from the major industrial nations. This could illuminate many things about the management systems and internationalization strategies of different countries, with their potential weaknesses. For instance, Bartlett and Yoshihara (1988) argue that, because the Japanese system, based on *nemawashi* (consensus building) and *ringi* (shared decision making), depends on close physical proximity and shared cultural values, it is not easily sustained over a long distance except through large numbers of expatriates and frequent trips back to Japan ('jet age *nemawashi*'). This system, they argue, is therefore vulnerable to rising costs and the demand for expatriates outstripping supply.

The extent to which Japanese companies depend on an expatriate system is illustrated by two comparisons they make:

[Kao] has a cadre of sixty expatriate Japanese managers and technicians running overseas operations with only 2,000 employees. This is more than double the number of American expatriates its U.S.-based competitor Proctor and Gamble has in an international business with total sales over twenty times larger. More significantly, all of the top management positions in Kao's overseas companies and most of the level below that are Japanese nationals; in P&G only five of the 44 subsidiary general managers are American. A similar contrast can be made between Matsushita and 3M. The former has over 800 expatriates in an international business with 40,000 employees; the American company has less than 100 expatriates to manage its 38,000 employees.

(Bartlett and Yoshihara, 1988: 25)

What such figures do not tell us is whether these organizations are simply at different stages in their entry to foreign markets (that is, in the internationalization process). Systematic data of this kind, taking into account the stage of internationalization, could usefully underpin internationalization research in general. No such study appears to exist, however – certainly not tracking changes over time.

Expatriate failure

The subject of expatriates has nevertheless been a major focus of concern in the American human resources literature. American firms may rely on formal controls to a greater degree, and the numbers compared with those of Japanese firms may be fewer. However, the number of American firms operating abroad is considerable and the total of expatriates is, therefore, substantial. One estimate (Root, 1986) suggested that in 1976 there were around 100,000 American managers in subsidiaries of American firms abroad, and these managers naturally tended to occupy the key positions. However, these expatriate assignments also appear to suffer very high failure rates. Not unconnected with this is the fact that international assignments are not held in particularly high esteem as a necessary route to the top in American companies.

Mendenhall and Oddou (1985) estimate the expatriate failure rate to have varied between 25 and 40 per cent in the period 1965–85, while Desatnick and Bennett (1978) put it at up to 70 per cent in developing countries. This is considerably higher than the failure rate experienced among European and Japanese multi-nationals. Tung's (1982) survey found 76 per cent of US multinationals had failure rates of more than 10 per cent, compared with only 14 per cent of Japanese firms and 3 per cent of European firms. A recent survey of forty-five British and Irish multinationals by Scullion (1991) confirms this generally favourable situation (under 10 per cent of British and Irish firms reporting failure rates higher than 5 per cent). In a smaller sample of twenty-five European MNCs, Brewster (1991) found similar low rates of failure, although there was a marked discrepancy between the French firms (relatively high rates of failure) and the Swedish firms (low failure rates). This may be partly attributable to the industries in which national firms participated.

However, this should not, as Tung observes, obscure the fact that all multinationals have a problem, especially as failure at any level represents a serious problem both organizationally and for the individual careers of relatively senior employees. Financially also, any failure is serious. One UK company, for instance, has put the extra cost of servicing an expatriate at £40,000 annually. Moreover, as Scullion observes, defining failure in terms of premature return or recall before the completion of an assignment may overlook a willingness to countenance inferior standards of performance (or, indeed, the absence of adequate appraisal measures).

The importance of the topic is further underlined by the increasing use of expatriates among British and Irish firms, revealed in Scullion's study – two-thirds of which, out of a sample of forty-five firms, use expatriates to run overseas operations. Interestingly, this runs counter to American trends, where, for reasons of cost and politics and the difficulties they have experienced, American multinationals are cutting back on their use of expatriates. This may simply represent a necessary readjustment as American firms become less ethnocentric and more responsive to local conditions. On the other hand, some American commentators see in this trend a potential loss of strategic control (Kobrin, 1988).

If expatriation is an important topic, then, and expatriate failure is a significant problem, what are the sources of failure, or, conversely, the rules for success? There is a fair measure of agreement by now as to the principal causes of failure.

Including the family

The most frequently cited reason for an assignment ending early is the inability of the partner of the person concerned to adjust to a different physical or cultural environment (Tung, 1982). It is usually the partner and children who have to engage most closely with the host culture, including managing the local language, while they are most often left out of consideration at the time of selection and in preparing for the assignment. Of course, it may simply be expedient for the expatriate to blame their spouse, rather than to admit a failure to adjust themselves (Dowling and Welch, 1988).

In examining the psychological adjustment of the partner to relocation abroad, De Cieri, Dowling and Taylor (1991) conclude that it is important to consider the partner and family in the selection and preparation, and that one of the most useful contributions a company can make is in providing or developing a social support network in the host country to alleviate the stress which such relocation undoubtedly entails. Two of the chapters in Brewster (1991) are of particular interest in this regard in documenting the experience of expatriation from the point of view of the expatriate and their family, with the range of problems encountered and some suggestions for overcoming these.

Although a company may not actively consider the partner's wishes or concerns, in point of fact these may intrude quite considerably in the self-selection through which employees rule themselves out from overseas assignments. One survey of relocation just within the UK found, for instance, that 60 per cent of a group of managers had at one time or other refused a job move because of family commitments (IMS, 1987). The growth of dual career families, the difficulty for spouses to find meaningful work (Forster, 1991), and less willingness to disrupt children's education mean that relocation in general and international relocation in particular are becoming increasingly problematic. A partial way round such difficulties, which some companies like Shell are experimenting with, is to focus international moves on employees early and late in their careers, with a period of greater stability in the middle when they have school-age children and their spouses are building their own careers.

Selection

A second source of difficulty, very much mirroring those that concern the family, is the adjustment of the expatriate to the new setting. This derives, in the first instance, from the criteria for selection. Overwhelmingly, these are based on the person's technical competence to do the job, measured in part by a successful domestic track record and such factors as knowledge of the company's systems and procedures (Mendenhall and Oddou, 1985; Mendenhall, Dunbar and Oddou, 1987; Gertsen, 1990; Barham and Oates, 1991; Brewster, 1991). Clearly, technical competence is a *sine qua non* – the 'bedrock on which other skills must be founded' (Barham and Oates, 1991: 70). By comparison, the lack of attention given to relational abilities is notable (Tung, 1982).

The Ashridge survey reported by Barham and Oates (1991:102) reveals a particular discrepency in this respect between the importance managers attach to relational skills, such as 'adaptability to new situations', 'sensitivity to different cultures', 'ability to work in international teams', and 'relationship skills', and the criteria which win out when it comes to choosing managers to work abroad.

It is easier to state such requirements than to measure them, however. There is a considerable literature on personality traits and attitudes around these dimensions (see Gertsen, 1990), but as Gertsen notes, following Church (1982) and Ruben and Kealey (1983), 'the majority of these studies show relatively modest results when it comes to predicting a person's success in a foreign culture'. Indeed, certain criteria often assumed to be positive indicators appear on closer investigation to have a negative impact. This applies especially to how a person responds to 'culture shock'. The absence of culture shock might be taken to show a person's resilience. Studies of how expatriates react suggest, however, that culture shock is a positive experience (Hawes and Kealey, 1981; Ratiu, 1983). One explanation is obviously that if a person is immune to differences in culture, they are not sensitive in responding to them. A contrary problem is that exceptional sensitivity may mean an expatriate 'going native', and becoming less responsive to the requirements of the parent organization.

Besides 'relational skills', and in fact number one on the list of desired qualities in the Ashridge survey, is 'global awareness' – a strategic outlook which comprehends world trends in business. The aspect of this they stress is not what strategic analysis can reveal, but the curiosity and openness to look at the world at large for ideas, trends, possibilities, and examples of best practice. On closer inspection, in fact, this is another personal quality, rooted in a desire to know and communication skills.

A broad interpretation of 'inter-cultural competence', therefore, is that it comprises personality and attitude traits, knowledge and cognitive skills, and communication skills, including the behavioural skills that must accompany language ability (Gertsen, 1990). It is not just about personality and so-called 'behavioural skills', but an issue of cognitive style as well. An important part of how a person reacts in another culture is thus the way they interpret behaviour and evaluate individuals. With this in mind, Detweiler (1980) and Ratiu (1983) identify a readiness to categorize and form fixed judgements ('narrow categorisers') as characteristic of a less adaptive, more ethnocentric outlook.

However, as noted earlier, 'inter-cultural competence' is only part of the story. Decisions on expatriate management should take account of a range of issues to do with the person, and a range of situational factors, including job requirements, the setting the person is being transferred to, and family circumstances (Gertsen, 1990). A narrow concern with the qualities of the person is all the more misplaced insofar as many companies have a very limited number of people to choose from who are suitably qualified technically, or who can be spared from the home operation. In such circumstances, training and preparation become all the more important (Gertsen, 1990).

Preparation and training

After careful selection and the general principle of involving the family at all stages, the next major issue in successful adjustment is the help the company can give to prepare the assignee. Table 4.3 from the Ashridge survey identifies a number of helpful practices in this respect, with the frequency with which the organizations sampled use them.

Gertsen's (1990) survey of personnel managers in eighty Danish companies confirms that companies give most attention to language preparation and providing a preliminary visit to the

Table 4.3 Preparing managers for international postings

(% of respondents ranking an activity as among the five most important methods in their organization)	%
Arranging for managers to visit host country	79
Language training for managers	73
Briefing by host country managers	67
In-house general management course	44
Cross-cultural training for managers	42
Cross-cultural training for family	38
General management course at business school	29
Language training for family	23
Training in negotiating within business norms of host country	17

Source: Barham and Oates (1991: 166)

country in question (although the importance of these two activities is reversed in her sample). The provision of language training varies, however, between countries, with such evidence as we have suggesting that Swedish firms give a high priority to it, while American firms are less likely to (Baliga and Baker, 1985; Bjorkman and Gertsen, 1990). One interesting consideration is that the need for language training may vary between sectors, depending on the extent to which English is the international language. Thus, Brewster (1991) observes that in the airline and petroleum industries, English is the international language, and most employees who operate internationally will speak English as a matter of course. The same is true of banking to a lesser extent. Food and drink and electronics, however, have no common international language, and one would expect language training to be a greater requirement among all firms, including British ones.

As Table 4.3 indicates, training can vary considerably in depth. Landis and Brislin (1983) and Mendenhall, Dunbar and Oddou (1987) propose similar classifications for viewing training methods, according to low, medium, and high levels of rigour. These range from 'information-giving approaches', through 'affective (or behavioural) approaches' using devices such as role playing, to 'immersion approaches'.

Views differ, in particular, about the value of training, especially the utility of cross-cultural training, in advance of an assignment. Cross-cultural training has strong advocates – for example, Brislin (1981), and Landis and Brislin (1983). Above all, it develops self-confidence (Black and Mendenhall, 1990). This, it will be recalled, was cited in Chapter 2 as one of the key issues for the small firm entrepreneur in taking the first steps towards internationalization via exports. Top management, however, generally do not see pre-training as necessary, believing that learning cannot really occur until the person is in position abroad (Mendenhall and Oddou, 1985; Schwind, 1985; Gertsen, 1990). This parallels the wider debate about the value of pre-training versus on-the-job learning. Thus, Derr and Oddou (1991), in a sample of 135 individuals, mainly from the US electronics, banking, and defence industries, found that over 65 per cent had no preparatory training at all, while one-third simply received reading materials.

Despite this, specialist consultancies like Moran, Stahl & Boyer in the USA and centres that specialize in cultural training (such as the Centre for International Briefing, at Farnham Castle in the

UK) have been widely used by companies over many years. Japanese firms in particular are reported to approach cultural preparation with far more seriousness and rigour (Murray and Murray, 1985), including placing staff with English families to help with acculturization (John Foden, Chief Executive, PA Management Consultants, personal communication). Ronen (1989) advocates the wider use of this for in-depth preparation. Less thorough, but still effective, is for a person to begin to 'shadow' the overseas business they are to go to in a head office liaison role for a period in advance (Brewster, 1991: 61).

Above all, it is important that firms start to prepare staff well in advance of international assignments. Rothwell (1992) advocates at least a year, so that thinking internationally can become part of a continuous process, rather than preparation being condensed into a flurry of international briefings just before departure. This clearly depends on the much wider requirement, discussed below, that firms conceive expatriate activity within a framework of career management.

The important question for training in all this is what objectives it should have. Just as the desirable qualities to look for in selection closely resemble good people skills, so those that training should aim to develop are skills of generic application, not specific to international assignments. Thus, Harrison and Hopkins (1967) emphasize that training programmes should teach individuals how to learn, and Harris and Harris (1972) argue that one does not have to cross national borders to acquire cross-cultural experiences. The willingness to change one's own style of communication to suit a listener, for instance, is a sign of flexibility in any inter-cultural interaction – and in some home-country situations it may be just as essential to survival.

Opportunities for cross-cultural experiences and learning abound in any country with diverse religious, racial and ethnic groups, and in the possibilities to mix with groups differentiated by class, age, or sex:

> skills for global leadership may be quite generic in application to other management contexts . . . training programmes should attempt to impart generalizable skills by which individuals 'learn how to learn' in any intercultural setting and engage in team building activities with diverse individuals.
>
> (Lobel, 1990: 44)

In any case, in order to understand another culture, people may first need to understand their own and the processes which helped them to arrive at their particular set of values, beliefs, perceptions, and ways of behaving (Ratiu, 1983). Neale and Mindel (1992) used such a method in multi-cultural teambuilding at BP's Brussels-based finance centre by getting people to explore their own national culture as part of the process.

By the same token, as Rothwell (1992) comments, 'managers may learn more about a country from holidaying in it than from any jet-setting business trips, but little attempt is ever made to build on this'. In other words, it pays to build on 'ordinary' experiences in preparing people for international assignments.

Terms and conditions

After selection, preparatory training and the inclusion of the expatriate's family in these processes, the fourth area that expatriate management has to address are the terms and conditions under which a person goes abroad. For many companies, this is the major area of concern. Indeed, it often seems that for some companies their perception of what internationalization entails is entirely limited to problems in determining pay. This is a complex and highly technical area and companies that lack experience in this area would be well advised to make use of consultancies which specialize in advice on compensation packages for expatriates.

Dowling and Schuler (1990) have a useful chapter on the subject which shows the range of issues that have to be taken into account and elements of the total package that have to be reconciled. The crux of the issue is, first, maintaining relativity with domestic colleagues and protecting the terms of domestic contracts (such as pensions), while second, providing motivation for the inconvenience of relocating abroad and compensating for the discomforts of particular locations. Reynolds (1986) has argued for a 'balance sheet' approach as a way of reconciling the various elements of compensation and satisfying these objectives. This is described in Dowling and Schuler (1990: 118–20). The 'balance sheet' incorporates the two main methods otherwise used to determine pay – the 'build-up' method, which adjusts the expatriate's equivalent home salary and benefits according to cost-of-living indices and exchange rates; and the 'host country' system, which compensates for local market conditions.

The guiding principles are that expatriate compensation, like compensation generally, has to be perceived as fair and equitable (taking into account the whole range of national differences in basic levels of pay, taxation, side-benefits, pensions, and so forth); it has to be presented in a clearly understood form; and it has to be controlled so that the company does not end up paying inflated rates which encumber it as international activity grows (Barham and Oates, 1991: 174). As we have indicated, the cost of international assignments has become the principal concern of American firms (Schuler and Dowling, 1988).

Managing careers

Dowling and Schuler (1990) amplify many of the issues around the management of expatriates, and their book represents an excellent primer on the subject. However, one area that is curiously under-developed in their treatment is the place of expatriate assignments in careers. The career issue features briefly in relation to repatriation problems which firms encounter (pp. 61–3). Equally, though, it should be a consideration in the preparation phase, in dealing with the expectations of employees. In other words, expatriate assignments need to be viewed as part of a career process – a series of work-role transitions (Forster, 1992) – and managed through a career system which integrates domestic and international requirements. This issue takes us on to the second level of internationalization, whereby career management becomes increasingly significant as the firm's involvement in internationalization deepens.

Organizations encounter two problems with expatriates which implicate their career systems (or lack of one). First, is the difficulty they often have in finding suitable people to choose from in making international assignments. Second, is the problems they have in fitting them back into the organization to the employee's satisfaction and to the advantage of the company. In large part, this is an issue of maturity in making international transfers, as we implied earlier in relation to the internationalizing firm. The newly internationalizing firm lacks critical mass in the numbers of employees undertaking international assignments and therefore has difficulty managing flows out of and back into domestic operations. While these difficulties concern the integration of international and domestic career management, they may also reflect on the adequacy in general of an organization's career management.

The kind of general problems which expatriates encounter have been consistently documented (Torbiorn, 1982; Adler, 1986; Tung, 1989; Derr and Oddou, 1991). They include

- being forgotten once out on assignment;
- becoming disconnected from the power system, decision making centres, and corporate succession plans;
- returning to less challenging jobs.

In a study of 135 American repatriates, Derr and Oddou (1991) found that the effects on careers were generally felt to be negative, even though those managers surveyed were mostly all regarded as high performers in their performance evaluations. Not surprisingly, therefore, American firms seem to have difficulty retaining repatriates. A survey by Moran, Stahl and Boyer (1989) of fifty-one top US firms, for instance, found 45 per cent had difficulties retaining repatriates; while a survey by Korn/Ferry International (1986) of 1,362 senior executives found less than 1 per cent said that a career in the international business was a fast route to the top.

These responses seem to reflect more on the attitudes of American companies than those of European firms. One explanation for this is that the domestic American market is much more important as a source of revenue and business for most American firms than are their home markets for European and Japanese firms (Tung, 1988). As a result, international assignments have acquired a bad image among American managers and among MBA students, which bodes ill for the future (Adler, 1987). By contrast, Barham and Oates (1991: 108ff.) provide a number of examples of European firms that have a well-integrated approach to the development of international managers. However, such 'best practice' examples may be misleading about general patterns, and we lack detailed evidence about how satisfactory are the career management practices of UK and other European companies generally towards expatriates. Certainly, some UK firms do have difficulty accommodating returnees (Johnston, 1991).

The management of repatriates focuses a number of issues to do with firms' career management systems. Analysing the attitudes of top American firms to international assignments and training,

Derr and Oddou (1991), for instance, find that in most cases the companies' own complaints about expatriates reflect adversely on the way the company itself conceives of international assignments and weaknesses in its career system. Those firms with ineffective expatriate–repatriate practices tend to share the following characteristics:

- There is a failure to regard international assignments as developmental, leading to top management positions, nor do they regard international know-how as a source of competitive advantage.
- Selection is not backed by a strategic human resource planning process that identifies needs and ensures, in turn, that re-entry is to positions identified some while in advance.
- Preparation is sporadic.
- Support while away is negligible.

One specific way in which companies' career management systems may be failing is in their inability to make effective use of women, both as a general resource for international assignments and for the particular qualities they can bring. Jelinek and Adler (1988) argue, for example, that women in international management can draw on

> characteristics that have traditionally been a fundamental part of the female role in many cultures – their great sensitivity, communication skills, and ability to establish rapport. Women need not buy into the competitive game. They can subtly shift the interaction out of the power and dominance modes so typical of business interchange – and so dysfunctional in cross-cultural relations – into the sort of cooperative, collaborative modes becoming increasingly important today.
>
> (Jelinek and Adler, 1988)

Barham and Oates (1991: 78) also observe that women's skills at networking could be particularly relevant insofar as internationalization itself is a networking process.

One other sidelight on the neglect of women for international positions is that the prejudices in certain countries such as Japan against promoting women may offer incoming multinational companies a ready source of educated talent that they can recruit for their own operations (Dowling and Schuler, 1990: 65).

Management development systems may also lend themselves to particular kinds of internationalization strategies. Evans, Lank and

Farquhar (1989), Evans (1990), and Dulfer (1990), for example, imply that the functionally-oriented development of specialists in the German system is more adapted to an export-led strategy, whereas the generalist system that is characteristic of Anglo-Saxon, Dutch and Scandinavian firms is particularly suited to transnational operations. Rapid progress through a variety of jobs in different functions, locations, and businesses produces a cadre of people able to manage a diversified international company. By the same token, although these authors do not suggest this, the 'political tournament' which characterizes the promotion system in 'Latin' firms such as the French may discourage overseas assignments because the manager is out of sight and therefore less well-placed to compete for attention.

These suppositions obviously depend on national stereotypes. Moreover, just as with the suggestion that Japanese firms may have difficulty managing overseas operations in the longer term through the vulnerability of their management system to the cost of sending expatriates (Bartlett and Yoshihara, 1988), there is an element of whistling in the wind at the supposed weaknesses of the two strongest economies in the world. The serious question, nevertheless, is what kinds of qualities and behaviours management development systems promote, and how well-adapted these are to the particular international strategy a company may be pursuing.

Finally, the trend towards shorter overseas postings of two to three years raises an important point which unites considerations of strategic control with that of management development. As Brewster (1991: 38) notes, more frequent, shorter assignments may be less efficient, since it takes time to gain a clear grasp of an overseas situation and to feel confident to take important decisions. At the same time, stability in the overseas subsidiary depends substantially on the second tier of local managers. Their influence and ability to block unpalatable decisions increases the shorter the tour of duty of the visiting expatriate. This depends, however, on a particular scenario in the use of expatriates (PCN) *vis-à-vis* local management (HCN).

Internationalizing the organization: the role of corporate culture

The consideration of expatriates and career management thus far has had an implicitly ethnocentric character. As the BP example illustrated, however, the more thoroughly international a company becomes, the more power becomes spread, the more it draws on multiple centres of expertise, and the more the career system is characterized by two-way movements. At the same time, the more complex the organization becomes, the more its integration and cohesion is seen to be dependent on cultural norms, and less on formal structural controls through reporting relationships. At this point, then, attention shifts to broad educational efforts to internationalize the organization at large, and this may include creating a common framework of organizational culture:

> Attention in recent years has been focused, with varying degrees of success, on integrating the decentralized firm in more soft and subtle ways – first, through programs to create an over-riding corporate culture, and second, through international executive development.
>
> (Evans, Lank and Farquhar, 1989: 117)

Thus, the movement of employees ('international executive development') contributes to the creation of corporate culture by spreading corporate values. In this connection, Barham and Oates (1991) stress the need for top managers to make themselves seen around the globe in the various business units, while inter-nationalizing the composition of management (especially at director level) is also important for practical and symbolic reasons.

Of primary importance, however, are the organizational values themselves and the means by which these are expressed. Evans, Lank and Farquhar (1989: 118) assert that there are five elements in the creation of a corporate culture:

1 a clear and simple mission statement;
2 the vision of the chief executive officer;
3 management education;
4 project-oriented management programs;
5 the process of building a corporate charter.

However, as they acknowledge, corporate culture is a controversial concept.

For instance, the relevance and impact of corporate mission statements may be questionable, while 'despite the fashionable concern with the vision of the "transformational leader", large international firms question how powerful this is in securing integration, since the CEO is a distant figure for most employees' (Evans, Lank and Farquhar, 1989: 119). On the other hand, management education whose content is made more international is likely to have a positive impact. Similarly, as in the BP example, management secondment into teams with a project-orientation is at the same time a vehicle for promoting culture, and an expression of the very type of culture which the transnational requires. It thus supports the view contained in Evans, Lank and Farquhar's (1989) last proposition that it is the process above all which is important in developing an international corporate culture (irrespective of the particular point about its role in building a corporate charter).

Bartlett and Ghoshal (1989), in their idea of building commitment by 'creating a matrix in managers' minds', and Barham and Oates, likewise stress the promotion of core values that managers in particular can identify with around the world. As Barham and Oates (1991: 46) put it, 'a clear philosophy and values provide[s] a strong context in which people can plan and act'.

However, there is a basic irony and contradiction in all of this about corporate culture, because it runs contrary to the basic premise of the transnational as an organization seeking to benefit from international diversity. The very idea of 'the corporate culture' conjures up the classic image of the MNC that Schneider, for instance, deplores:

> an international cadre of executives . . . corporate mercenaries . . . corporate soldiers [trooping from country to country] through frequent and multiple transfers designed to encourage the loss of identification with their country of origin and its transfer to the corporation. . . . In these global 'clans', corporate identification may come to override community and even family identification.
>
> (Schneider, 1988: 244)

In other words, a strong corporate culture belongs to an ethnocentric world-view, where control and values are determined centrally in the parent country. The issue for the transnational – the truly internationalized company – is therefore 'what kind of corporate culture?' There seem to be three positions on this:

1 Corporate culture is seen as a cultural export to bend people to doing things in the same way;
2 Corporate culture is seen as the best amalgam of national differences, which is then made into the corporate culture;

3 The corporation takes national differences seriously and allows them to have expression. In effect, this is the antithesis of corporate culture – the corporation accepts differences as an article of faith.

The second of these approaches has a way of resulting in the creation of a new monolith, and is essentially unstable except in very limited circumstances (as in the Anglo-Dutch corporations, such as Shell). The real choice is therefore between 1 and 3; behind this choice is the whole question of which is the more powerful influence on individual behaviour – national or corporate culture?

On the one hand, there are those who see behaviour as constrained by elements of organization, such as size, product environment, and technology, and by the managerial imperatives of control and coordination (Horvath, McMillan, Azumi and Hickson 1976; Negandhi, 1979; Hickson, McMillan, Azumi and Horvath, 1981). These contingencies are seen as prime determinants of regularity in behaviour across organizations, and therefore the organization's control of these factors enables it to impose a degree of behavioural conformity on employees. The proponents of this view may be termed 'culture-free' theorists (Axelsson, Cray, Mallory and Wilson, 1991). On the other hand are those who take a 'culture-bound' view, that organizations are shaped by individual preferences which are themselves shaped by society (Hofstede, 1980, 1991; Lincoln, Hanada and Olsen, 1981). Behaviour within this context is the expression of individuals' cultural differences within a socially 'congenial' environment.

The well-known, pioneering work of Hofstede (1980) provided a timely and powerful affirmation of national differences against the background of a world apparently moving towards dominance by large corporations. Taking IBM, a company notable for having a powerful corporate culture, as his 'control', Hofstede surveyed the attitudes of IBM employees in fifty countries, and found systematic differences between nationalities on four dimensions ('power distance', 'collectivism/individualism', 'feminity/ masculinity' and 'uncertainty avoidance'). By contrast, organi- zation culture often operates at a relatively superficial level on behaviour, finding expression principally in symbols, heroes, and rituals (Hofstede, 1991).

The validity of national stereotypes is also questionable,

however (Conrad and Pieper, 1990). The issue, as Laurent has observed, is not simply the 'mean' of attitudinal measures, but their distribution. A range of positions allows for an overlap between the attitudes of individuals from different cultures, and this makes convergence and common work possible. Nevertheless, Hofstede's findings have been corroborated in one or two focused, in-depth studies. For example, in their study of decision-making styles in British and Swedish organizations, Axelsson, Cray, Mallory and Wilson (1991) found differences between the two countries around the individualist/collectivist and feminine/masculine dimensions, in line with those in Hofstede's IBM survey.

Over a number of years, Andre Laurent (1986: 93) has surveyed managers participating in executive programmes at INSEAD on a great number of measures, including Hofstede's dimension of attitudes to power, authority and hierarchical structure, and concluded similarly that 'the most powerful determinant of their assumptions was by far their nationality'. Extension of this work to a single American multinational, in the manner of Hofstede, produced a similar picture of cultural differences unaffected by the organization. Other studies by Trompanaars and the EMF Foundation, reported in Hampden-Turner (1990), show similar differences around the attachment to hierarchy.

Such national differences have significant implications in terms of motivation to work (Adler, 1986), willingness to take risks (Cummings, Harnett and Stevens, 1971), interpersonal skills (Bass and Burger, 1979), speed of decision making and the search for consensus (Harper, 1988; Heller and Yuki, 1969, Axelsson, Cray, Mallory and Wilson, 1991). Whereas the 'corporate culture' concept slides over these differences, the 'national differences' perspective says it is necessary to recognize these and work with them.

The problem, as Laurent (1986) and Adler and Jelinek (1986) observe, is that the concept of organizational culture is itself peculiarly American. It embodies American cultural norms of dominance and free will, doing and achieving, that express themselves in a belief in being able to control and manipulate the natural world:

Fundamental to the organisation culture concept is the belief that top management can create, maintain, and change the culture of an organisation . . . . Management's influence is seen as capable of changing or erasing other influences on employees' behaviour. Similarly, work environment influences are seen to dominate private life conditioning . . . . Moreover, employees are seen as capable of changing; and change, in and of itself, is basically good.

(Adler and Jelinek, 1986: 82)

Laurent (1986) suggests, instead, that it would be more realistic to reserve the term 'organizational culture' to the more superficial layers of norms and expectations, and the behaviours that sustain these. Adler, Doktor and Redding (1986) likewise argue that the formal aspects of organization, like structure, may, indeed, become similar, but people's behaviour at the 'informal' level will continue to show culturally-based dissimilarities. The implication is that the so-called 'matrix in managers' minds' is an illusion not worth pursuing. Effort would be better expended in raising levels of understanding of international colleagues in different settings, as in preparing for an international assignment.

As Hofstede (1991: 237) observes in his latest work, a sense of personal identity, based in the value standards of one's own national culture, is essential for intercultural relations, because only in that way can one have the feeling of security to encounter other cultures with an open mind: 'one does not need to think, feel, and act in the same way in order to agree on practical issues and to cooperate.' By contrast, the most problematic nations, groups, and individuals to deal with are, first, those who score very high on the 'uncertainty avoidance' measure, lack openness, and feel that 'what is different, is dangerous'; and second, those who score very high on 'power distance', which puts up barriers to cooperation.

In conclusion, the approach of most companies to internationalizing the organization through a reliance on management education, personal meetings and international seminars (Derr and Oddou, 1992) is not, in the end, too wide of the mark. Raising the level of understanding of international colleagues in different settings is the basis of successful intercultural relations. A cosmopolitan international management development programme (at a venue outside the parent country) is probably therefore one of the first and most important steps an organization can take towards becoming more fully international.

As an organization grows more comfortable and familiar with

running such events, national differences within the organization can themselves become a focus for review. In doing so, however, it is more important to look at the way national behaviour is structured by institutional, belief, and economic systems, rather than to become fixated on the psychological and attitudinal dimensions that tend to predominate in research studies (Hendry, 1991). In other words, it is necessary to look at socialization processes, rather than to treat behaviour as genetic. In doing so, the scope of the organization in influencing behaviour can come into more effective focus.

This is an important issue in the design of HRM systems and practices themselves, since HRM systems represent the major interface between corporate ideas of behaviour and its individual expression. Chapter 6 on comparative HRM systems will pick up this theme.

MANAGING COMPLEXITY IN THE INTERNATIONAL FIRM: THE SKILLS OF MANAGERS

At the outset, following various authors, we stated the problem of the international firm as one of managing increased complexity. The idea of the transnational presents this in particularly stark form, where it is expected to develop simultaneously the characteristics associated with the MNC, global and international firm. The dominant firm of the future must sense needs in one market, respond with capabilities perhaps developed in a second (geographical or product) market, and diffuse any resulting innovations to markets and facilities around the globe (Bartlett and Ghoshal, 1989). The crux of this is a need to manage both external and internal complexity.

This obsession with bigness and complexity may in the end be self-defeating and beyond the capacity of any business organization. The transaction cost argument suggests that some tasks are better left to external market relationships and structures. Indeed, the whole point of Bartlett and Ghoshal's thesis is that existing approaches to coordination were beginning to founder in the 1980s in the face of these emerging challenges (1989: 166). Neither the characteristic Japanese approach to coordination that they found, nor the American approach, nor the European approach, were without problems, especially in the costs they entailed.

Such characterizations, based on the study of just nine companies, may be simplistic. Goold and Campbell's (1987) study of strategic styles, for instance, suggests greater diversity. Nor is Bartlett and Ghoshal's remedy – 'building commitment' – a convincing advance historically on existing systems. It is not clear how this is different, for instance, from Unilever's socialization/career management system which they describe; as we have seen, the idea of building commitment has a major contradiction at its heart.

Nevertheless, the problem posed remains undiminished – 'Increasingly, the management of complexity, diversity, and change is the central issue facing all companies' (Bartlett and Ghoshal, 1989: 198). Or as Doz and Prahalad (1986: 55) put it, organizations have a problem in managing 'controlled variety'. Ultimately, this comes down to the skills of managers. What is this 'management of complexity', though? What does it involve, and can it be learnt?

One of the most penetrating analyses of what is involved comes from Weick and Van Orden (1990). Defined in terms of learning theory, the problem is one of 'equivocality' of information – too much conflicting, ambiguous and unstructured information. This contrasts with the problem supposedly faced by organizations in the past, that of uncertainty and ignorance arising from lack of information. Examples of equivocal problems are whether or not to make an acquisition, what corporate goals to set, and where to locate R&D activities:

> questions of this kind can be answered only through interpretation, judgment, building a common perspective out of conflicting views, defining both the problem and what constitutes an acceptable answer, exchanges of information and experience, and the enactment or construction of solutions rather than the discovery of pre-existing solutions.
>
> (Weick and Van Orden, 1990: 52)

Such problems are made more manageable when the richness of data increases. While information technology has been highly successful in reducing ignorance and uncertainty, it is ill-adapted to the criteria for effective communication in processing 'rich' information. The forms of communication which score best in dealing with these problems are face-to-face, personalized settings. As a result, small groups and teams provide the ideal forum for communication on global issues, because potentially they can include sufficient internal diversity to match the diversity of the environment they are trying to deal with.

However, the existence of a group and diversity within it are no guarantee of coping effectively with complexity. This depends on trust, honesty and mutual respect among members. This is where organizational values and socialization come in. Common organizational values (with the reservations previously stated) provide a 'strong organisational context' (Barham and Oates, 1991) in which trust can flourish. Likewise, common socialization develops a basis of tacit and implicit knowledge which can help teams to function more smoothly:

> The organisation's style, values, traditions, and leadership are critical encouragements to the cooperation and commitment of its members. These can be viewed as intangible resources which are common ingredients of the whole range of a corporation's organisational routines.

> (Grant, 1991: 122)

The first stage of Weick and Van Orden's argument, then, is about the importance of teams for sense-making in global management. Others have reached similar conclusions about the importance of teams to large organizations generally, while emphasizing the importance of networking in building the interpersonal relationships on which subsequent team-formation depends (Kanter, 1989; Bartlett and Ghoshal, 1989). Learning theory thus provides a sophisticated rationale for organizing in teams.

The second stage of their argument is about the process for addressing global issues. Because these are characterized by equivocality, it makes sense to tackle issues in small portions, or small portions of issues, in order 'to create pockets of order' in the face of global turbulence: 'Action facilitates learning in nonroutine settings and small wins get people into action more quickly' (Weick and Van Orden, 1990: 55). As others have argued, incrementalism can result in the accumulation of sequences of successful operational acts of adjustment, from which a sense of the bigger, strategic picture can materialize (Whipp, 1991).

This emphasis on incremental learning, like the importance of networking inside the organization, leads to an important insight – namely that key issues and skills in the internal management of the global firm, involving teamwork, incremental learning, and networking to manage complexity, are the same as those for managing the process of internationalization externally. Or as Bartlett and Ghoshal (1989: 199) put it, 'the task of managing across corporate boundaries has much in common with that of managing across national borders'. Apart from elements of knowledge relating to the different environments, basic skill development need therefore not differentiate between internal and external processes. Rather, recognition of these as common and important processes should produce a sharper focus on the elements of skill involved.

Weick and Van Orden (1990) set out four requirements for such skill development. First, they list a number of relevant skills: negotiation; initiating and managing change; coping with overload; self-management; construction of processes; communication; improvisation; sensemaking; persuasion; and representation of complex systems. Second, they specify five areas where people need to develop particular understanding. These concern

• the effects of overload and uncertainty on individuals and groups;
• how knowledge is organized and modified;
• coping with organizational politics;
• alternative forms of organization; and
• the nature of meaning-interpretation systems.

Third, for purposes of learning, these skills and knowledge need to be applied to specific contexts and issues in the business curriculum. And fourth, the learning unit for all this, whether in the business school or in the organization, should be teams.

Business schools in both the USA and Britain, however, are largely seen as not having provided companies with suitable support on internationalization, especially in managing process issues. Weick and Van Orden's characterization, emphasizing process skills, is therefore timely in this respect. On the other hand, process skills in the management of complexity are likely to be highly context-specific, and therefore not readily 'teachable' outside the international firm. Employers' expectations of international business programmes tend, in fact, to be rather muted and appear to recognize that companies in some respects are better equipped to develop what they want: what they seek, first and foremost, is able people (Beamish and Calof, 1989).

Part of the problem is the extent to which the growth of

international business has run ahead of the perspectives and resources of the higher education system. It was with such problems in mind that the Swiss business schools, IMI and IMEDE (now merged as IMD) were originally set up by international companies. More recently, business schools in America and Britain have been making strenuous efforts to internationalize themselves. Barnett (1990) sets out the requirements for this as follows:

- cultural exposure through international internships and student exchanges with other universities and businesses world-wide. Much more flexibility in terms of experiential course credit;
- language programmes for students and faculty;
- comparative courses in all disciplines;
- teams as learning units to develop skill sets useful in global organizations. Team building within culturally diverse student groups, using overseas students and faculty as country 'experts' to enliven the cultural dimension of case studies;
- new visiting faculty recruited from foreign countries for collaborative research and teaching;
- establish exchanges with foreign universities and global corporations;
- problem-centred courses taught by faculty from multiple disciplines, with business executives participating regularly to make inputs on international themes;
- courses focusing on particular applications instead of generic skills to develop 'global leadership', and a curriculum which develops the skills and addresses the problem areas that Weick and Van Orden identify;
- courses that draw on the interdisciplinary strengths of the entire university;
- development of non-traditional teaching methods appropriate to the 'new knowledge' triggered by the globalization of business.

A survey of twenty British business schools by Arkin (1991) shows that students value an international student body above all else, since this ensures that an international perspective is brought to learning experiences such as case analysis. In this respect, European business schools have a natural advantage over American ones, and Continental European schools have an advantage over UK ones because of the diversity of the student population (Tully, 1988). Arkin's survey shows UK schools internationalizing themselves through a variety of means which meet many of Barnett's criteria. These include:

- an international student population;
- an international faculty (although this is inevitably slow to assemble);
- student exchanges;
- joint ventures with overseas institutions;
- foreign language options in the programme;
- an international curriculum (through cases and project work – although there is a dearth of cases with an international dimension);
- research that addresses international issues;
- governing bodies with an international character.

Most business schools, however, still do not make language teaching central to their programmes, although the former polytechnics tend towards this more than the older universities.

One other finding from Arkin (1991) is that pressure for internationalizing business schools comes from individuals looking for international careers, rather than from companies. This fits with a general pattern of companies recruiting people initially for their technical skills, preferring to develop the skills for internationalization in-house, and believing that certain of these have necessarily to be acquired in-company because they are specific to their particular markets and organization style. Company programmes for developing the skills of international managers are therefore of central interest, but inevitably highly diverse. Some examples can be found in Barham and Oates (1991). In this chapter, we have concentrated instead on some of the generic characteristics of skills and attitude they need to develop.

CONCLUSION

Alternative structures and trends in organizing for international business, deriving from competitive conditions and strategic responses, provide the starting point for understanding HRM in the international firm. Porter's distinction between markets which are multidomestic and those that are global is a key discriminator for the form which HRM takes. Alongside this is the degree of socio-cultural and legal differentiation, and the level of political and economic risk (Brooke and Remmers, 1970; Schuler, Dowling and De Cieri, 1993). Such factors determine how far human resource policies themselves are differentiated.

The result is a tension between centralization and decentralization in managing organizations. In recent years, decentralization has certainly been more in vogue (Hendry, 1990), although at any point in time one will also find a large proportion of firms reorganizing to strengthen central control (Lester, 1991). International firms increasingly seek to combine the benefits of both centralization and decentralization.

To illustrate this, the BP example showed how the UK's largest company has changed its structure over the years to manage an increasing complexity of operations and a changing portfolio of products and markets, and what this has meant for staffing policy and the management of international employees. We then analysed in some detail the HRM issues involved for firms at different stages of their international development. Longitudinal analysis of this kind of changing patterns in firms' policies towards internationalization is unusual, however.

As UK and European firms develop increasing variability in their international strategies and use of expatriates (and as the meaning of 'expatriate' in the European context, indeed, changes), we can expect a growth in European research in a field which has until recently been largely dominated by American work and perspectives. The multiple sources which Brewster (1991: 15–18) draws on represents the beginnings of such a data base.

The three principal themes in international HRM – managing expatriation, creating appropriate career systems, and internationalizing the organization through a corporate culture – are all about creating a cohesive and effective organization. The managerial task then comes down to one of managing complexity. This says little, however, about learning from internationalization (although the discussion in Chapter 3 on alliances had something to say on this). We shall pick up this theme in Chapter 6.

Chapter 5

Internationalization and the Single European Market

From general issues of internationalization, we turn now to the specific context of the Single European Market (SEM). Although companies must necessarily remain concerned with world markets, the SEM will increasingly dominate the experience of internationalization among UK and European firms. The reasons for this range from the formation of pan-European firms, to the impact of EC employment legislation and European comparisons on skills and training. As a result, both the international firm and the 'domestic' firm will be affected.

In this chapter we will review the impacts of the Single European Market on the industrial structure of Europe in general and of the UK in particular. In Chapter 6 we will then consider the implications for HRM.

THE SINGLE EUROPEAN MARKET AND INDUSTRIAL RESTRUCTURING

The completion of the Single European Market (SEM) at the end of 1992 gave new impetus to internationalization and to the restructuring of the world and European economies. The Single European Act of 1986 which set this process in motion aimed to remove trade barriers to the movement of goods and resources across the frontiers of the EC's member states, in three ways:

1 removing direct, physical obstacles to trade (customs controls);
2 lowering non-tariff constraints (the differing technical standards and regulations governing goods and services);
3 equalizing price distortions from the varying rates of indirect taxes (VAT) and excise duties.

The common European Exchange Rate Mechanism (ERM) was also intended to contribute to a 'level playing field' by reducing the scope of member countries to vary the exchange rates of their currencies. As we know, however, this has run into some difficulties because it tried to produce a convergence in currencies while there remain large underlying disparities in economic development.

All of these initiatives directly impact upon international (intra-European) trade by companies domiciled within the Community. The result will be a vast, unified market with a population in excess of 320 million, which will stand comparison with and provide a formidable challenge to the market of 243 million in the USA and 122 million in Japan (along with the new 'tiger economies' of South-East Asia). The Single European Market will therefore realize the image of a world economy dominated by the 'triad power' of these three great trading blocs (Ohmae, 1985).

The removal of these barriers is expected to produce a once-and-for-all boost to trade and efficiency as the SEM is completed. However, in the longer term, realizing the benefits of the SEM will require the exploitation of scale benefits, and that implies major restructuring of European industry. At the same time, European firms are expected to engage in closer cooperation to develop their technological competitiveness and market strength *vis-à-vis* the USA and Japan. The SEM is thus expected to stimulate three processes (Directorate-General for Economic and Financial Affairs, 1988; Cecchini, 1988; Emerson *et al.*, 1988; Ramsey, 1990):

- internal restructuring and rationalization to refocus (that is, standardize) products in an extended internal market;
- external restructuring through mergers and acquisitions, to gain the advantages of scale;
- cooperation through joint ventures, pooling of R&D resources and expertise, and other forms of alliance to improve technology.

Beyond the removal of trade barriers in the ways indicated, the EC has been developing policies to directly assist restructuring, standardization, and cooperation among European firms. These include:

- the involvement of EC firms in the preparation of new industrial standards;
- preferential access to public procurement contracts (Directorate-General for Economic and Financial Affairs, 1989: 56–63);

- subsidies for investment and research, and collaborative European programmes in high technology (ESPRIT, BRITE);
- specific policies for encouraging SMEs (Commission of the European Communities, 1989).

Instances of the latter, such as the European Information Centres and BC-NET, have already been mentioned. Other intiatives within the programme for SMEs include the 'European Economic Interest Grouping' facility, which is intended to facilitate cross-border alliances among SMEs (Tigner, 1990).

Restructuring

The process of restructuring which the SEM is intended to stimulate was already well under way by the late 1980s. Well-publicized acquisitions, mergers, and alliances have taken place in the pharmaceutical, food, defence (Farr, 1989; Evans, 1990) and aerospace industries (Martin and Hartley, 1991), with continued major restructuring anticipated in motor vehicles (Sasseen, 1989) and telecommunications (Parry, 1990), among others. Deals involving chemicals, food and drink, and the paper/printing industry have recently accounted for more than half of all cross-border acquisitions within the EC, while these sectors along with metals and electrical engineering have seen most of the large deals (Commission of the European Communities, 1991).

However, partnerships that fall short of being outright mergers have been spread across many sectors. Companies domiciled in non-EC European countries such as Sweden and Finland have also been active in seeking partnerships outside their own territory, while over a third of partnerships in the latter part of 1989 were based on Eastern Europe. In Sweden's case, a small domestic market and exclusion from the EC have long since encouraged an international orientation and this has led to considerable acquisition activity within the EC. In the run-up to 1992, this accelerated and foreign direct investment in the EC by Swedish companies increased by 50 per cent from 1987 to 1988.

As Figure 5.1 shows, the number of mergers and acquisitions within the EC increased consistently through the 1980s, from around 150 in 1983/84 to nearly 500 in 1988/89. During this period, the growth in transnational mergers between industrial companies across European borders is particularly striking. Inward investment (by countries such as Japan and the USA) also accelerated as the prospect of an exclusive SEM – or 'Fortress Europe' (Kaikiti, 1989) – neared, with a high proportion of this investment targeted on the UK.

On the other hand, while mergers in the service sector have grown at a similar rate overall, the numbers involved are fewer (at around 175 in 1988/89) and are more domestic in character. Recent service mergers are also dominated by the banking and insurance sector.

Latterly, however, after four years of growth, the trend in international mergers and acquisitions has reduced sharply. According to figures from KPMG (Peat Marwick McLintock), the value of international takeovers fell from £117.8bn in 1990 to £51.9bn in 1991, as recessionary economic factors asserted themselves. Acquisition activity in Europe showed a similar sharp decline, with UK activity particularly falling away (Peat Marwick McLintock, 1991).

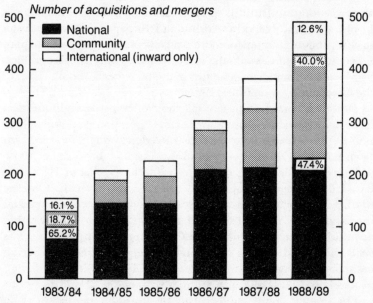

Figure 5.1 Mergers and acquisitions in the industrial sector in the Community (1983/4 to 1988/9)
Source: Directorate-General for Employment, Industrial Relations and Social Affairs (1990: 50)

Despite such cyclical factors, these figures are an indication of the European Commission's goal of larger companies being realized. They also show, however, that European industrial restructuring is being driven not simply by takeovers among European firms, but through takeovers of indigenous companies by foreign (American and Japanese) capital. International realignment and restructuring has been going on for some time, while acquisitions and mergers are part of a normal competitive process, with acquisition a preferred route to quick market entry (Curhan *et al.*, 1977; Yamin and Batstone, 1987). For such reasons, many regard 'Europe 1992' as a relative sideshow to the real continuing dynamic of international competition:

> One might be surprised that we did not mention the Single European Market (1992) as one of the driving forces of industry dynamics in the 1990s. The reason is simple: for most of the managers [in the study], the Single European Market (SEM) will not be a crucial force in the evolution.
>
> Broadly, the impact of the Single European Market is very different across industries, and for most of the businesses it is just an accelerating force among others in the dynamics of internationalisation. While most of the managers speak about the psychological, indirect impact of 1992, many of them think it is a non-event. . . .
>
> The political changes in Eastern Europe, thought to herald major economic changes, are perceived as at least as important as the Single European Market.
>
> (Calori and Lawrence, 1991: 138, 178)

Cooperation and competition

Alongside these processes of agglomeration and rationalization, the European Commission is also seeking to promote cooperation and encourage smaller firms. Some commentators therefore argue that EC policies on competition and cooperation are fundamentally at odds. The attempt to intervene in these conflicting processes may also be harmful and misguided.

The principal moving force in the SEM programme was to restore the economic dynamism of the EC (to overcome what had become known as 'Eurosclerosis'), by stimulating trade and improving the technological progressiveness of EC firms. This was to be achieved by increasing collaboration and promoting cooperation. This theme was prominent, for example, in the EC White Paper (Commission of the European Communities, 1985), and in the subsequent Cecchini report and research studies which attempted to set out the benefits and likely effects of a Single European Market:

> Europe-wide standards . . . are an essential lever for prising open national markets and then welding them together through technological alliances. Of great importance to such alliances are EC-sponsored R&D programmes like ESPRIT which, way beyond their monetary significance, are a crucial focus for fusing cross-frontier innovation and business.
>
> (Cecchini, 1988: 89)

Kay (1990), however, argues that (i) the evidence Cecchini relies on for companies cooperating is flimsy; (ii) collaboration is in fact more common between EC companies and non-EC companies than between those in member countries (being especially pronounced in the critical high technology sectors of chemicals, electrical products, mechanical engineering, and computers); (iii) companies in any case do not willingly enter into joint ventures except as a last resort; (iv) full mergers and exporting are likely to be preferred strategies in the completed open market; and (v) these restructuring effects will tend to reduce competition. Even one of the EC's own studies (Geroski, 1988) suggested that it is competition that leads to increased innovation, rather than collaboration.

Kay draws three conclusions from this. First, a strong merger policy is necessary to limit anti-competitive mergers and acquisitions. Second, science and technology policy should not seek to concentrate resources, nor support groups of cooperating firms. And third, schemes to promote cooperation between SMEs run against the grain of other aspects of EC policy. Others put more emphasis on the relationships between large and small firms in localities (the 'industrial districts' model). Thus, Cowling (1990) argues that economic dynamism depends on relatively small firms within supportive regional structures, while Cooley (1989) relates this to the argument for flexible production systems based on a skilled workforce.

The European Commission has not been unaware of these conflicts, however, and has always seen exploiting the opportunitites of the SEM as the result of diverse strategic decisions by companies

(Directorate-General for Economic and Financial Affairs, 1988:132). Since September 1990, the EC has finally had powers to control cross-border mergers, and the peaking of mergers and acquisitions in early 1990 and their subsequent decline may in part be attributed to the adoption of these powers (Commission of the European Communities, 1991), although recession, high interest rates, and problems of company liquidity have also been major factors.

The effects of policy have also been subject to closer and continuing investigation as the SEM has become more of a reality through harmonization and the progressive enactment of the 279 intended directives governing industrial standards. Thus, one of the criticisms of the Cecchini report and the full study (Commission of the European Communities, 1988a) was that it considered only the aggregate impacts. This omission is now increasingly being made good at the sectoral level (Directorate-General for Economic and Financial Affairs, 1990; Bowen *et al.*, 1991; Calori and Lawrence, 1991; Pescotto, 1992), and regional level (Begg and Mayes, 1991; Dunford and Kafkalar, 1992).

The sectoral impacts of the Single European Market

Sectoral-level analysis suggests that the SEM is likely to impact especially on some forty manufacturing sectors where there are significant non-tariff barriers to intra-Community trade (Buigues and Ilzkovitz, 1988; Directorate-General for Economic and Financial Affairs, 1988). These forty sectors represent about 50 per cent of industrial value-added in the Community out of a total of 120 such sectors. At the same time, industrial goods as a whole account for around 70 per cent of trade both within the Community and with the outside world. Thus, although the forty manufacturing sectors are not of absolute significance to the European economy, they are critical in the impact that reducing barriers will have in stimulating trade within the SEM.

The Directorate-General, Economic and Financial Affairs (1988) classified these into four groups (as shown in Table 5.1) according to the level of price dispersion that identical products display across member states and the level of intra-Community trade. These two measures show how fragmented the EC market is for each sector and how severe the effects of harmonization are therefore likely to be.

Table 5.1 The industrial sectors most affected by the Single European Market

NACE Codes	Sector	Non-tariff barriers
	High-technology public-procurement sectors	
	Group 1	
330	Office machines	high
344	Telecommunication equip.	high
372	Medico-surgical equip.	high
	Traditional public-procurement or regulated markets	
	Group 2	
257	Pharmaceutical products	high
315	Boilermaking, reservoirs, sheet-metal containers	high
362	Railway equipment	high
425	Wine & Wine-based products	high
427	Brewing and malting	high
428	Soft drinks & spa waters	high
	Group 3	
341	Electrical wires & cables	high
342	Electrical equipment	high
361	Shipbuilding	high
417	Spaghetti, macaroni, etc	high
421	Cocoa, choc. & sugar confec.	high

continued

NACE Codes	Sector	Non-tariff barriers
	Sectors with moderate non-tariff barriers	
	Group 4	
	Consumer goods	
345	Electronic equipment	moderate
346	Domestic-type elec. appl.	moderate
351	Motor vehicles	moderate
438	Carpets, lino, floor cov.	moderate
451	Footwear	moderate
453	Clothing	moderate
455	Household textiles	moderate
491	Jewellery, goldsmiths' & silversmiths' wares	moderate
493	Photog. & cinemat. labs	moderate
495	Games, toys & sports goods	
	Capital goods	
321	Agric. machin. & tractors	moderate
322	Machine tools for metals	moderate
323	Textile & sewing machines	moderate
324	Machines for footstuffs ind.	moderate
325	Plant for mines, etc.	moderate
326	Transmission equipment	moderate
327	Other specific equipment	moderate
347	Lamps & lighting equipment	moderate
364	Aerospace equipment, manuf. and repairing	moderate
	Intermediary goods	
247	Glassware	
248	Ceramics	moderate
251	Basic indust. chemicals	moderate
256	Other chemical products for industry	moderate
431	Wool industry	moderate
432	Cotton industry	moderate
481	Rubber industry	moderate

Source: Panorama of EC industry and estimates from Commission Services/ Directorate-General for Economic and Financial Affairs/Employment, Industrial Relations and Social Affairs (1990: 24)

For instance, high price dispersion in Group 2 industries is due directly to non-tariff barriers created by public procurement policies (pharmaceutical products, railway equipment) or by the existence of national or regional standards (brewing and malting) which restrict cross-border trade. A number of Group 2 industries are characterized by national champions and may already have achieved high levels of concentration within national borders as governments have sought to gain internal cost advantages and/or to protect these industries against outside competition. The impact of harmonization will be greatest on this group, leading to restructuring, gains in technical efficiency, a narrowing of price differences, and growth in intra-EC trade.

Group 3 is similar to Group 2 in having high non-tariff barriers. However, it has relatively low price dispersion, as a result of generally higher levels of trade within the EC and, in most cases, higher levels of extra-EC trade (electrical equipment, shipbuilding). The expected impact of the internal market is in the same direction as for Group 2, but will be much less severe.

In Group 1, the considerable openness of the EC market to outside import/export trade has tended to level out price differences despite non-tariff barriers. High levels of national concentration may again exist. The reasons for this vary, but include the need for scale in R&D in technologically competitive industries. In these sectors, the higher ratios of imports to the EC over exports point to serious productivity disadvantages in the face of multinational (US and Japanese) competitors. These sectors are therefore regarded as competitively weak (office machines, telecommunications equipment). The internal market will act as an incentive to restructuring and cooperation (so the Commission hopes), giving economies in R&D effort, production and distribution. The prospect of strong growth in demand in these sectors will help in the adjustment.

The large number of sectors in Group 4 are characterized by moderate non-tarrif barriers and high import penetration, but also high price dispersion. This apparent paradox can be explained in a number of instances by the role of product differentiation in consumer goods (motor vehicles, footwear, clothing). Since there are already high levels of intra-EC trade in these sectors, the impact of the internal market will be relatively slight on their production facilities, although there are expected to be impacts downstream on distribution networks which will feed back and influence price convergence. The EC's external trade policy is likely to be more important than the creation of the single internal market.

These impacts at the sectoral level have direct significance for HRM. First, the European Commission does not, in general, expect there to be major dislocation in economic activity across the Community:

> The completion of the single market should . . . neither upset the mix of sectoral specializations across Member States nor lead to massive transfers of economic activities between geographic zones . . . .
>
> [E]ven in some weak sectors of a Member State, there are dynamic firms which can export successfully . . . . The challenges that such Member States face are therefore not sectoral. Instead the outcome will depend on their firms' potential to adapt to a new type of business environment.
>
> (Directorate-General for Economic and Financial Affairs'
> 1990: 4/5/51–2)

This suggests that HRM at the company level, with all that that entails, may be at a premium. On the other hand, it is unduly sanguine about how adequate and relevant are national systems of education and training for the development of skills that firms need to draw upon.

Second, the assessment at sectoral level confirms the assumptions about an increase in firm size as the basis for internationalization. If acquisition is the route to this, as it seems to be, it raises questions about firms' ability to manage the difficult process of mergers and acquisitions – especially where these cross borders.

Third, the Directorate clearly looks forward to the development of European firms. However, there is still an observed tendency in most developed countries of the Community to favour partnerships between national firms to give them critical mass to match firms in other member states – in other words, to bolster national champions. There are thus few genuine European firms with comparable market shares in each of the member states (Directorate-General for Economic and Financial Affairs, 1990: 5). Among the means for creating genuinely European firms are the promotion of managerial mobility and the need to establish cross-national representation on company boards. These and other factors in the creation of European firms have profound implications for HRM in terms of the national differences HRM accommodates and the development of a European model of HRM.

Chapter 6 will explore in detail these three themes for HRM. Before doing so, however, we will review some of the more precise characteristics of the UK industrial structure and of UK firms compared with other European countries, to understand the scale of the challenge facing the UK competitively and the EC in creating a genuine Single Market.

STRUCTURE AND STRATEGY IN THE UK AND THE EUROPEAN COMMUNITY

Against the European background, what are the particular characteristics of UK industry and firms? For example:

- What is the size distribution of UK firms, compared with other European countries?
- How do trade patterns compare?
- What are the patterns of outward investment?
- What are the patterns of inward investment?
- What are the employment consequences of investment patterns?
- How does productivity compare on a sectoral basis?
- How does profitability compare as a measure of company strength?

We consider these under three headings – the degree of industrial concentration, comparative levels of internationalization, and the extent to which this internationalization is focused on Europe.

Industrial concentration

As Table 5.2 shows, the UK has more employment concentrated in large firms and small–medium enterprises, as against micro-firms (less than ten employees), than the Community as a whole, while Germany also has a much larger SME sector (Bannock and Partners 1990). This disparity is especially marked in manufacturing, where the UK also has a much smaller proportion employed in both SMEs (10–499 employees) and micro-firms.

Another way of looking at this is in the numbers of very large

Table 5.2 Percentage of number of enterprises and of employment by size, class and sector (1986)

	Micro		SME		Large	
	UK	E-12	UK	E-12	UK	E-12
Enterprises:						
All	90.09	91.34	9.74	8.56	0.18	0.10
Manufacturing	81.13	82.70	18.07	16.91	0.80	0.39
Construction	93.88	91.28	6.06	8.68	0.06	0.04
Services	90.47	93.03	9.42	6.92	0.11	0.06
Employment:						
All	23.17	26.89	46.80	45.02	30.03	28.10
Manufacturing	6.92	11.14	38.83	45.95	54.26	42.91
Construction	43.05	39.53	43.49	50.57	13.47	9.90
Services	30.02	34.75	52.45	43.44	17.53	21.82
	1–9		10–499		over 500	
			Number of employees			

Source: Bannock and Partners (1990: 6.8)

firms on a country-by-country basis. Thus, the UK has 40 per cent of the top 500 industrial companies in the EC in terms of sales, compared with Germany which has 16 per cent (Lloyd, Carton-Kelly and Mueller, 1991). This dominance is reflected similarly whether one takes all EC firms with over 1,000 employees and subsidiaries in at least two member states (38 per cent of the 880 such firms are UK-based), or the largest 100 (48 per cent are from the UK) (Sisson, Waddington and Whitston, 1992).

The relative importance of smaller firms in Germany (a strong economy) as against the UK (a weak economy) should cause us to hesitate, therefore, at the European Commission's proposal that greater industrial concentration will be a good thing. This neglects the actual contribution of the SME sector to European economies and particularly its dynamic relationship with larger firms. Renewed interest in the idea of 'industrial districts' suggests the critical factors in dynamic, internationally competitive industries are (i) the existence of a constellation of firms of varying sizes in customer–supplier relationships, (ii) who operate in close proximity, and (iii) who compete with one another (Porter, 1990). One of the things this sustains is a more vibrant market for skills.

While the UK is highly polarized in the size and importance of the large corporate versus SME and micro sectors of the economy, as compared with France and Germany, there is also little interpenetration or integration between the two (Lane, 1991). In other words, certain of the essential conditions for a dynamic economy are absent.

In terms of national product, a similar picture of polarization emerges, with UK SMEs contributing 32 per cent of private sector GDP, compared with 46 per cent in Germany (Bannock and Albach, 1991). Table 5.3, using a different definitional base, likewise shows the UK's largest companies providing almost twice the proportion of GDP as equivalent-sized German firms. If we ask, however, which country benefits more, we observe first that the respective economies of the UK and Germany account for 15 per cent and 25 per cent of European GDP (Lloyd, Carton-Kelly and Mueller, 1991: 26), and second that the UK, with its economy dominated by very large companies, is near the bottom of the league in terms of GDP per head of population. In other words, German economic strength rests on a wider company base, and the German economy is better served by this more even spread. The comparison with Denmark is even more pronounced, Denmark being the most prosperous and yet one of the least industrially concentrated member states.

Table 5.3 Prosperity and corporate concentration

Country	GDP Ecu bn	GDP/head Ecu 000s	Companies listed	Total sales Ecu bn	Sales % GDP
Denmark	97.8	19.1	15	18.9	19.3
Germany	1,111.1	18.2	81	507.5	45.7
Luxembourg	6.0	16.0	1	5.2	32.5
France	886.7	15.8	111	427.9	48.3
Belgium	145.9	14.7	17	48.8	33.4
Italy	831.6	14.5	25	98.8	11.9
Netherlands	208.6	14.1	35	166.2	79.7
UK	686.4	12.1	201	573.2	83.5
Spain	346.4	8.8	10	20.5	5.9
Ireland	31.3	8.7	4	4.9	15.7

Source: Lloyd, T., Carton-Kelly, A. and Mueller, M. (1991) 'EC Heavyweights', *International Management* April: 26. Based on data supplied by Extel Financial's MicroEXSTAT European statistical service.

International companies

The UK already has the most internationally-oriented economy in the EC, as a result of acquisition activity by British firms abroad and foreign investment in the UK, and until the recent recession depressed activity, the UK continued to be at the forefront of this process. Figures for 1988/89, for example, show British firms as being far and away the most active in mergers and acquisitions, accounting for 60 per cent of total transfrontier deals, compared with the French at 23 per cent, the Dutch at 5.5 per cent, and German and Italian firms at 3.5 per cent each (Directorate-General for Economic and Financial Affairs, 1990). Eighty-five per cent of this activity by British firms, moreover, was in the USA. In the case of mergers and acquisitions among industrial companies within the EC, the UK was just behind France, but closing rapidly at the end of the 1980s (see Figure 5.2).

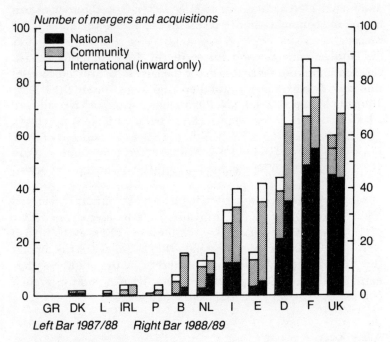

Figure 5.2 Mergers and acquisitions in the industrial sector in the member states (1987/8 and 1988/9)
Source: Directorate-General for Employment, Industrial Relations and Social Affairs (1990: 52)

Numerous studies suggest, however, that mergers and acquisitions perform less well as a whole than companies pursuing a strategy of organic development (Fairburn and Kay, 1989; Cutler *et al.*, 1989). The performance of British firms in consequence has been generally depressed by past waves of merger activity (Kitching, 1967; Cowling *et al.*, 1980; Lubatkin, 1983). When this process, which has not been particularly successful domestically, is translated into a means of internationalization, the degree of acquisition/merger activity clearly poses a major challenge for UK and other European firms.

As a result of the level of outward investment, UK firms are among the most internationalized in the EC in terms of where their employees are located. ILO figures for the early 1980s cited by Ramsay (1990) show UK multinationals on average have a much higher proportion of employees abroad (40 per cent) than German, American, and Italian multinationals (all at 25 per cent), and French MNCs (20 per cent) (UN, 1988). Only those with small domestic economies, like Switzerland and the Netherlands, have more.

Coupled with the job losses in the UK from the 1980–2 recession, the result is that many of the largest 'British' companies now actually have a majority of their employees outside the UK. By 1987, for instance, ICI, GKN, Pilkington, Turner and Newall, and Glaxo had joined five others (BAT, before its break-up, BOC, Lonrho, Beecham, and RTZ) with more than 50 per cent of their workforce overseas. By 1989, Williams, Williams and Haslam (1989) report this figure applied to eighteen of the top 100 British firms.

Moreover, as a result of UK investment patterns oriented towards North America, UK firms are relatively absent from the list of Europe's biggest domestic employers. Thus, only British Aerospace and GEC, plus the Anglo-Dutch Unilever, rank among the EC's top twenty-five manufacturers in the numbers they employ in Europe, compared with nine German and five French companies (Labour Research Departments, 1989).

A European economy?

The European Commission saw mergers and acquisitions as a necessary step towards creating strong European firms. As we have seen, however, UK acquisition activity in 1988/89 was more oriented to North America than to Europe, and this was part of a long-standing pattern through the 1980s. The result appears to be that UK firms, and the UK economy as a whole, are less European than global.

In terms of exports certainly, as Table 5.4 shows, UK companies are more oriented to markets outside the EC than are all other EC countries, except Denmark, although the proportion of UK trade within the EC has been increasing since Britain joined the Community in 1973. Given that the aim in creating larger European firms is to strengthen their competitiveness internationally and to promote European trade with the rest of the world, this is a positive sign. From this, we might conclude that the UK is well-placed – better than almost all other EC countries – to exploit markets outside the EC.

A critical issue, however, is the substitutability of exports by foreign direct investment, and central to this is the quality of firms' exported goods and export strategies. Studies by Oulton (1990) and Williamson (1990), for instance, cast doubt respectively on the quality of British firms' exported goods and their commitment and approach to exporting. In the long run, fundamental weaknesses of this kind are likely to encourage globally-oriented British firms to transfer activities to overseas production and to substitute overseas investment for exports. The shift in employment by UK firms during the 1980s to subsidaries abroad shows that this is precisely what has happened.

The result is a vicious circle, as far as indigeneous skills are concerned. On the one hand, as Oulton (1990: 25) observes, 'the ability to manufacture and export sophisticated, high quality

Table 5.4 Percentage of exports to EC countries

	%		%
Denmark	48.5	Greece	68
Great Britain	49.4	Portugal	71
Germany	53.1	Ireland	74
Italy	56.6	Belgium/	
		Luxembourg	74.5
France	60.4	Netherlands	75.1
Spain	63.8		

Source: OECD/Calori and Lawrence (1991: 12)

products rests on possession of a [domestic] work force plentifully endowed with skills'. On the other, however, the high dependence within the British training system on large firms for the development of these very skills means that if they withdraw activity from the UK, the whole skill base suffers (Keep, 1992).

The result then is high import penetration and greater exposure of the UK market to foreign investment (although there are clearly other factors in the eagerness of foreign firms to invest in the UK). The substantial trade deficit, and in particular the imbalance with Germany, which accounts for around half the UK's total £10–24bn annual deficit over the six years 1986–92 is one measure of this. The other is the stock of foreign direct investment. As a proportion of GDP, this is around 23 per cent in the UK, compared with 7 per cent in both Germany and France, and 4 per cent in Italy (Directorate-General for Economic and Financial Affairs, 1990). Only the Netherlands has a higher proportion (at 36 per cent). Throughout the post-war period, the UK has been the largest European recipient of American and Japanese investment. In other words, the pattern of inward investment confirms the 'global' rather than specifically European character of UK-based firms.

Both inward and outward investment and employment patterns show, then, why the UK is a strong supporter of an 'open door' policy on trade and investment within the EC. When taken with evidence on the internationalization of UK R&D (Cantwell, 1990), British-owned firms are among the most internationalized in Europe. In turn, this highlights important differences in business culture between the UK and the other major EC countries. In Germany and France (not to mention others like Switzerland), there are strong institutional constraints to mergers and acquisitions generally and to acquisitions by non-indigeneous firms in particular. In these heartland economies of Europe, therefore, there remain powerful barriers to the formation of European firms.

CONCLUSION

The creation of a Single European Market is undoubtedly a major event in international business, although how it ranks as compared with the creation of a private enterprise system in Eastern Europe and the former Soviet Union, or with the emergence of China as a world economy, or the continued rapid evolution of South-East Asia's 'tiger economies', is more contentious. What distinguishes the Single European Market from a human resources point of view is, first, the specific encouragement to form European firms through pressures to rationalize in an enlarged 'domestic' market, and second, the attempt (muted though it is) to achieve a convergence on skills, training, and employment conditions. These present specific challenges to HRM and raise questions about the convergence of European models of personnel management towards a single European model of HRM.

For instance, while the European Commission's goal of larger companies is being realized, there is, on the positive side, considerable potential for the transfer of best working practices. On the negative side, there is the difficulty of reconciling different company cultures and the national differences in which these are embedded. As the European Commission observes:

> Quite considerable numbers of employees are being affected if only by changes in the pattern and structures of ownership of their employers. This may lead to changes in work practices as the products and services supplied change, as investment increases and as management styles alter.
>
> This may require considerable effort in the fields of human resource management and vocational training in order to ensure that the mergers are successful.
>
> (Directorate-General, Employment, Industrial Relations and
> Social Affairs, 1990: 50)

Alongside this European perspective, there remain nevertheless chauvinistic sentiments about the effectiveness and future of industry in each country. UK comparisons with our EC partners, for instance, show that:

• The UK has the highest level of industrial concentration in the EC;
• The UK has the most internationally-oriented economy, as a result of its export orientation, the acquisition activity of British firms abroad, and investment by foreign firms in the UK.

These do not seem, however, to have delivered national prosperity and industrial competitiveness. One of the aims of the next chapter is to review the specific human resource factors in this.

Chapter 6

The Single European Market and the HRM response

In this chapter we consider three themes. First, we review the impact of the Single European Market on employment in Europe and the response at national level in terms of skills and training. We also briefly consider the use of the Social Chapter to mitigate national and regional disparities. Second, we look at the response at company level, especially at how employees are being affected by the formation of 'European' firms. The European Commission has tried to exercise some influence here, through measures designed to encourage employee mobility and the creation of a European labour market. Third, we consider the issue of convergence towards a European model of human resource management. This is a complex and intriguing question which exposes national differences rooted in institutions and culture, as well as the potential of international firms to spread best practice in technology and HRM. It is the same issue in the European context as the general one of how far international firms can transcend national cultures by imposing a distinctive one of their own.

At the heart of these themes is a critical duality – the need to even out some of the differences and disparities within the EC as a condition of reinvigorating the European economy. The Single European Market can only fulfil its aim of stimulating growth if the member countries can all feel they have something to gain. This means lifting up the laggards to the standards of the best. To that extent, the interests of the member countries may override those of international companies. On the other hand, the engine for growth is these same international companies. There is potentially, then, a conflict between different sets of economic and political interests that will require careful management. HRM is at the centre of this in the intersection of national and company-level issues of skills, training and labour mobility.

EMPLOYMENT AND SKILLS IN THE SINGLE EUROPEAN MARKET

From the outset, it was anticipated that there would be an initial loss of around a quarter of a million jobs across Europe for the first two years after the completion of the SEM, as administrative barriers came down. Restructuring and the boost to trade were then expected to result in a net gain of between 1.8 and 5.7 million jobs after six years (Commission of the European Communities, 1988). In these assessments, the UK was projected to suffer the most severe job losses (0.64 per cent, compared with an average loss of 0.44 per cent), and to have the smallest net gains (1.39 per cent compared with an average 1.47 per cent across the EC). However, as Ramsay (1990: 13) comments, 'the loss of jobs is the most secure thing about 1992; and the subsequent gain in employment is the least reliable'. Rajan (1990) concurs with this view in his assessment of the SEM as a 'zero-sum game'.

At a macro-level, the Institute for Employment Research at Warwick University has projected the effects of three possible scenarios on employment (IER, 1991). An 'efficiency' scenario, resulting from vigorous product-market competition and increased labour market flexibility, suggests an increase of 1.1 million jobs by the turn of the century – largely in service industries and in part-time, low-paid jobs. A 'cost-cutting' scenario, where there is fierce price competition between European competitors, would effectively negate these benefits and affect jobs in services and certain areas of manufacturing. A 'quality' scenario, in which Europe moves towards a high added value/high skill economy, would double the benefits and produce employment increases, especially in chemicals, construction and banking. The European Commission is implicitly committed to the achievement of this third scenario – a high added value/high skill economy embracing all of Europe.

Until recently, the European Commission continued to assume a modest impact on employment from the initial rationalization accompanying the SEM – noting in 1990, for instance, that, 'the process of completing the Internal Market is taking place against a background of relatively strong output growth and even stronger job creation' (Directorate-General, Employment, Industrial Relations and Social Affairs, 1990: 44). This view has, of course, since been revised to take account of the increase in unemployment (Directorate-General, Employment, Industrial Relations and Social Affairs, 1991). More especially, the Commission recognizes that any real assessment of the long-term effects needs to focus on impacts and responses at sectoral and regional level. It is here that any divergence will be most marked.

Sectorally, analysis has revolved round the forty manufacturing sectors most likely to be affected (see Chapter 5 and Table 5.1). Mapping these on a regional basis, the Commission distinguishes fairly crudely between the northern and the southern states. In the northern states, those among the forty sectors most likely to be affected tend to be capital-intensive high-tech (cars, pharma-

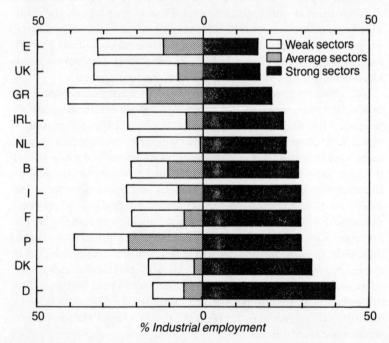

Figure 6.1 Share of industrial employment in sensitive sectors in the member states (1987)
Source: Directorate-General, Employment, Industrial Relations and Social Affairs (1990: 48)

ceuticals, computers, telecommunications) and traditional heavy industries (electricity-generating plant, railway rolling stock). Both of these are often protected by public procurement policies. In the southern states, those affected are likely to be labour-intensive industries such as clothing, footwear, textiles, ceramics and toys. Again, these also have been highly protected. Figure 6.1 shows the relative concentration of the forty most affected sectors according to their relative strengths and their importance to employment in the twelve member countries.

The Commission's overall assessment of the affects on the UK is actually somewhat contradictory. One report first observes that the share of industrial employment concentrated in the poorly-placed compared with strong sectors is greater (25 per cent, as against 18 per cent), but then qualifies this by noting that the larger proportion of total employment is concentrated in averagely performing sectors (Directorate-General for Economic and Financial Affairs, 1990:34). On this basis, the UK has a reasonably balanced distribution of employment. However, Figure 6.1 and the report from which it is taken presents a less favourable picture, with only around a third of UK industrial sectors competitively strong. With more weak and averagely performing sectors than most other EC countries, the UK is therefore in a similar position to Spain and Greece.

The inference is that the real gainers from the SEM, able to exploit the relatively strong position of their industries, will be Belgium, Denmark, France, Ireland, Italy and the Netherlands, which have proportionately more strong, as against weak, sectors – and Germany, where the share of well-placed sectors is highest and the share of poor or average-performance sectors is lowest. Thus, Germany has 73 per cent of its employment in strong sectors, and this in turn represents 40 per cent of total industrial employment. The positive and negative effects will cancel themselves out for Portugal and Greece. Taking the EC member states as a whole, therefore, the employment consequences for the UK are among the least favourable.

At one level, the issue is how member states respond and how through the 1992 programme the European Commission can help to bring about structural change in order to confound these predictions. For the southern states, this means either specializing in the same kind of products as now but improving their competitiveness on world markets – which carries the disadvantage that this will lock them into slowly growing markets – or becoming less dependent on basic industries like clothing and footwear, and achieving an industrial structure more like the northern states. Spain seems to be moving down this path. The challenge facing the northern states, on the other hand, according to the Commission, is to respond to international competition in their high-tech and industrially advanced sectors, while, at the same time, smoothing the shift out of declining heavy industries into growth sectors (Directorate-General for Economic and Financial Affairs, 1990: 47–8). At another level, bearing in mind the Commission's observation that even in disadvantaged sectors there are firms which are successful, the issue is how individual firms respond.

In either case, the key is capital investment in new production techniques and products, expanding the base of technological knowledge, and developing a more highly skilled workforce. Running through the Commission's programme for the SEM is thus a commitment to enhancing technological progressiveness and a belief that upgrading skills through increased training and development is essential:

> The importance attached to an education-training drive is not equally shared throughout the Community. Yet such a drive is essential as it must make it possible to renew existing qualifications, increase comparative advantages in terms of the ratio of real salary/level of qualification and therefore stimulate other types of investment (that is, not concentrated solely on industries with a high labour content).
>
> (Directorate-General for Economic and Financial Affairs, 1990: 99)

Other commentators have reached similar conclusions about the need to follow a high-skill strategy (Rajan, 1990; Lane, 1991).

The response to the SEM through skills and training

The Commission sees primary responsibility for raising skills lying with member states. Its own role is confined to (i) improving the level of basic education in certain states, such as Portugal and Greece, and (ii) spreading scarce skills more efficiently across the Community.

Although OECD (1989) figures show the stock of people in the UK with degrees is among the highest – if not the highest – in

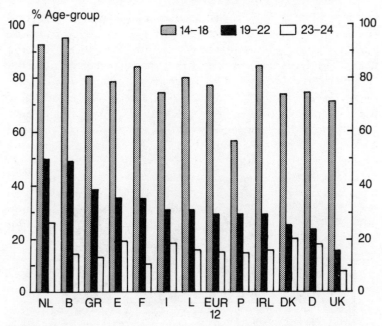

Figure 6.2 Share of young people in education in the member states
(1988)
Source: Directorate-General for Employment, Industrial Relations and Social
Affairs (1990: 113)

Europe, the participation rate in advanced secondary education
and FE/HE in the UK has been among the lowest in the EC and
OECD countries (Rajan, 1990: 179, 223) – as Figure 6.2 shows.
These figures are affected, however, by such factors as the length
of degree courses, which tend to be shorter in the UK. Moreover,
there has recently been a drive to achieve a substantial increase in
the number of students in higher education in the UK, and in
1991–2, numbers expanded from 14 per cent to 25 per cent of
school leavers.

The importance of basic and advanced education lies in the
throughput to firms. Clearly, any weaknesses here among member
countries will become a major stumbling-block in sustaining
existing high-tech/knowledge-based sectors and shifting more
traditional sectors onto a similar footing. Equally important is the
extent of post-school training young people receive alongside
those who pursue higher education. Figure 6.3 shows that the UK
lags considerably behind Germany, France and the Netherlands,

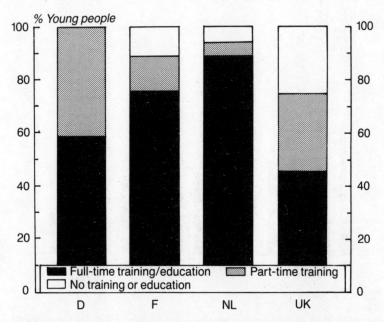

Figure 6.3 Proportion of young people receiving post-compulsory education or training by the age of 24 in some member states
Source: Directorate-General for Employment, Industrial Relations and Social Affairs (1990: 115)

with only 77 per cent of its young people in formal training or education beyond the school-leaving age, compared with virtually 100 per cent for Germany.

Figure 6.4 reinforces the picture of an underskilled workforce in the UK, in what is in effect its economic base, in the numbers and proportions achieving craft-level qualifications. Equally, the numbers obtaining a technician qualification in 1985 in the UK at 80,000 contrasted with 140,000 in France and 185,000 in Germany.

Other failings of the British educational and training system include the narrow base of skills and knowledge developed in training, which limits employee flexibility, and the separation of roles in the system, as between employers and educational establishments (Esland, 1990; Rajan, 1990). The latter problem, however, is not confined to the UK, and considerable efforts have been made in the UK in recent years to overcome this. (For a

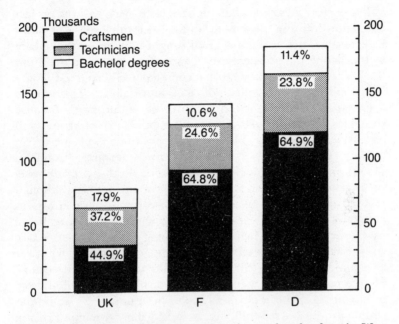

Figure 6.4 Number qualifying in engineering and technology in West Germany, France and the UK (1985)
Source: Directorate-General for Employment, Industrial Relations and Social Affairs (1990: 116)

review of reforms to the training system in the UK and comparisons with the training systems in Germany, the USA and Japan, see Hendry, 1993).

Systematic data on how far Community countries are responding to the call for an education-training drive is beginning to emerge from the Price Waterhouse/Cranfield Project (1990). One major problem, however, is that cross-country comparisons are bedevilled by different institutional systems. Company expenditure on training, for instance, reflects differences in who trains (companies or the state); whether or not there is legislative compulsion (as in France); and simply how efficient companies are at accounting for training. As studies of vocational education and training (VET) in Britain have shown (Pettigrew, Hendry and Sparrow, 1989), there is enormous variability in what activities are counted as training and what elements of cost are taken into account. Holden (1991) confirms that this problem is not confined to Britain.

Moreover, only crude attempts have been made so far to project education-training responses at the sectoral level. The joint Directorate-General report (1990) sought to open up the debate by translating the prospects for groups of sectors – and therefore the kinds of business strategy that companies will need to follow – into implications for policies on skills and training. This level of aggregation, however, is too broad to be useful, partly because strategies for same sectors will differ between countries (and companies), according to how they are positioned in those.

Neither the first report from the Price Waterhouse/Cranfield (1990) project nor Holden (1991) drawing on that provide systematic data as yet on sectoral expenditure and trends (although Holden makes some broad comparisons over where European countries concentrate spending). We cannot therefore judge whether countries are investing in training in those sectors where they have a comparative advantage, or, indeed, whether companies are trying to upgrade skills in threatened sectors. Should policy makers then attempt to pick winners in allocating, or encouraging the allocation of funds to training? Or would this simply produce a self-fulfilling cycle and deny dynamic firms in unfavoured sectors the opportunity to flourish?

One of the few studies so far to try to throw light on such questions is Boyce's (1992) study of the food and drinks processing industry in the UK, France and Germany, which found the level of training had yet to respond to the SEM. Others, such as Wood and Peccei (1990) in their case studies of the furniture and insurance sectors, have confined their analysis to one country and/or to an assessment of broad HRM responses. The latter is particularly interesting, though, in illustrating, through the differences in attitude and response towards the SEM, how the SEM is an extension of existing competitive dynamics within sectors.

In the furniture industry, for instance, the sample of twenty firms were almost exclusively oriented to the domestic UK market, to defending this, and to responding in short order to business threats and opportunities through short planning horizons. This behaviour reflects the fact that the industry is relatively fragmented. The twelve insurance firms were also relaxed about the implications of 1992 for their human resource plans, but for quite different reasons. In their case, there was already a strong

European connection, with all bar one having European interests. They were also more oligopolistic and comparatively strong, while the UK was thought to be unattractive to competitors because the market was relatively saturated. Therefore 1992 was seen as part of a long-standing Europeanization process, but further penetration into Europe depended on the speed with which EC regulations on finance and insurance were harmonized.

Since competitive profile, business strategies, and the impacts of harmonization differ markedly between sectors, so too will the relevant HRM requirements and preoccupations, as human resource strategies follow business strategies. Specific sectoral studies like this show the need for systematic studies which take account of size and sectoral factors, and, within these, the particular business and human resource strategies of firms which cause them to be positioned in Europe or not.

The most substantial effort so far to relate business strategy and the HRM response on a European sectoral basis is the study by Calori and Lawrence (1991) and colleagues of four sectors (brewing, retail banking, book publishing, and the car industry). They endorse the view that 'training will more and more be seen as a strategic weapon' (ibid.: 77), as well as identifying the importance of specific management qualities such as interpersonal and intercultural skills. However, even this does not provide precise evidence of actual company responses or how the behaviour of exemplary individual companies compares with sector norms.

To fill the gap at sectoral level, the European Commission has initiated a variety of programmes to analyse skill and training needs, and especially to identify skill shortages. These include COMETT (Community Programme in Education and Training for Technology) and FORCE (Continuing Training in Europe). Studies have also been undertaken into the electronics and textiles industries, and into the retail trade. Similar studies are in progress to analyse impacts and problems at regional level.

Skills, performance, productivity and pay

Although direct comparisons of skills are difficult to establish and we may lack data on current responses, it is clear that the UK falls short of the 'quality scenario' in two crucial respects – the level of wages and the level of productivity – which in turn reflect the skills,

Table 6.1 Labour costs and unit labour costs in the member states

	Labour costs	*Unit labour costs*
GR	– 56.1	– 24.4
P	– 74.4	– 13.9
I	1.4	– 11.8
E	– 25.8	– 11.4
F	18.4	2.9
NL	27.2	2.9
D	22.2	3.3
IRL	– 12.8	3.9
UK	– 23.0	7.2
B	17.5	7.9
DK	14.0	8.5
L	15.7	19.8

Source: Directorate-General for Economic and Financial Affairs/Employment, Industrial Relations and Social Affairs (1990: 88)

training, and the capitalization of its industry. As Table 6.1 shows, the UK ranks with Spain (plus Greece and and Portugal) in having lower than average labour costs per employee (wage plus non-wage costs). However, the UK also has above average unit labour costs, implying a lower level of capitalization than its principal north European industrial competitors, France and Germany. Putting these two statistics together, in other words, adds up to a low wage/low skill economy.

Comparative data on firms' performance and the way benefits are distributed reinforces this picture, while also revealing a striking contrast between the corporate philosophies which animate the economies of Europe. The analysis by Lloyd, Carton-Kelly and Mueller (1991) provides a devastating critique of UK national performance and the corporate values on which it rests. Taking the largest 500 European industrial firms as measured by sales (excluding those in the financial sector and utilities), they relate company profitability to the employee share of company wealth created. As Table 6.2 shows, the profit margins of large UK firms are much higher than those of their competitors on a company-by-company basis, higher across virtually all of eight principal sectors, and higher than the average, taking all sectors together.

Table 6.2 Sector margins in four EC countries

Sector	Italy %	France %	Germany %	UK %
Retailing	0.6	4.5	1.8	7.7
Food retailing	–	2.0	1.4	5.9
Motor/aerospace	11.5	5.7	5.7	6.4
Electrical/electronics	1.7	8.3	3.6	10.6
Engineering	5.0	5.0	4.2	9.3
Building materials	16.7	13.7	6.2	13.1
Chemicals/pharmaceuticals	7.2	6.7	7.2	15.3
Food/drinks	0.8	11.0	3.3	10.3
Average	5.4	7.1	4.2	9.8

Source: Lloyd, T. Carton-Kelly, P. and Mueller, M. (1991) 'EC Heavyweights', *International Management* April: 60. Based on data supplied by Extel Financial's MicroEXSTAT European statistical service.

There are institutional factors which go some way to explain this disparity – for instance, the need to cover for higher inflation and interest rates, and the reliance on retained profit as a source of capital. As Table 6.3 shows, however, this does not stop large UK firms from distributing more of the added value to investors and less to employees than large firms do in any of the other EC countries.

Table 6.3 Distribution of value added

Country	Companies listed	Investor share %	Employee share %
UK	201	8.1	60.2
Spain	10	8.1	65.6
Italy	25	7.3	64.1
Belgium	17	6.8	63.3
Netherlands	35	5.0	66.9
Denmark	15	4.3	69.8
France	111	3.7	69.2
Germany	81	2.7	75.7
Ireland	4	2.6	67.5

The rest of value added is accounted for by interest, tax and retained profit.

Source: See Table 6.2.

Thus, British firms have the highest profit margins, pay the highest returns to investors, and give the lowest share of added value to employees. This raises the question, 'which type of corporate culture will Europe follow in the future?' – 'Will it be the low-margin German pattern or the high-margin UK pattern? Or will the "European company" settle down to an intermediate margin closer to the French model?' (Lloyd, Carton-Kelly and Mueller, 1991: 60). Will it be one that rewards employees or investors? As they argue,

> Financial sophistication leads to greedy investors, low wages, lack of international competitiveness and, ultimately, a less prosperous economy. The *EC Heavyweights* analysis points to a link between the strengths of various economies and the generosity of companies towards their employees.
>
> It has always been assumed that high wages, such as those characteristic of Germany, are a result of prosperity, not a cause. The opposite may be the case. Countries with strong economies generally have companies that pay relatively large proportions of the value they create to employees, and relatively small proportions to investors. Companies in the Community's weaker economies are more likely to do the opposite.
>
> (Lloyd, Carton-Kelly and Mueller, 1991: 54)

Ireland's experience of multinationals tends to confirm this in the exceptionally low unit labour costs (or high level of profit per unit of value-added), which the high-tech multinationals based there achieve (Directorate-General for Employment, Industrial Relations and Social Affairs, 1990: 119). As critics of the European Community have long realized, increasingly internationalized economies require strong social controls – such as the Social Chapter is intended to provide – to prevent multinationals exploiting low wage economies. As a low wage economy and the most internationalized large economy in the EC, the UK is especially vulnerable.

The Social Chapter

The Social Chapter originated in concerns that the SEM might lead to regional polarization in the European economy, between high added value/high skill sectors (in the rich north and the 'golden triangle') and low added value/low skill sectors (in the south and peripheral areas). Low skill/low wage economies might then try to claw back their competitive position by what has become known as 'social dumping'. The Directorate-General defines 'social dumping' as follows:

'Social dumping' may be defined as a recourse to working conditions and social standards which are below the levels which the productivity of the economy could normally justify, with the purpose of increasing market share and improving competitiveness.

(Directorate-General for Employment, Industrial Relations and Social Affairs, 1990: 93)

The Social Chapter aims to discourage such actions as lowering wage costs, cutting social benefits, increasing hours of work, reducing restraints on employers, or lowering direct wages through a set of employee rights (combined with the use of the EC's structural funds to reduce regional disparities). Broadly, these cover twelve areas (see Hall, 1990):

1 The free movement of workers within the EC.
2 'Fair remuneration' for employment.
3 The improvement and approximation of conditions of employment.
4 Social security.
5 Freedom of association and collective bargaining.
6 Vocational training.
7 Equal treatment for men and women.
8 Information, consultation and participation arrangements.
9 Health and safety at the workplace.
10 Young people.
11 Retired people.
12 Disabled people.

Although the Charter was conceived with polarization between northern and southern Europe more particularly in mind, the concept is equally applicable to the UK, with its low wage/low skill economy. Moreover, as a highly internationalized, open economy, opposition to such controls can be seen as an invitation to 'footloose' multinationals to exploit the 'social dumping' possibilities.

The idea of the 'footloose' multinational, however, is no doubt overstated – certainly in terms of its desire to search out low-cost locations. As we have seen in earlier chapters, this provides only a partial account of the internationalization process. As Mosley

(1990: 161), for instance, notes, 'if labour costs alone determined international competitiveness there would be no industry in high wage countries'. This assumption of 'footloose' multinationals, otherwise known as the theory of the 'new international division of labour' (Froebel, Heinrichs and Kreye, 1980), has in general been quite heavily qualified (for example, by Elson, 1988).

Nevertheless:

> In so far as labour costs are one factor in competitiveness and social costs make up a significant share of labour costs, 'social dumping' will occur and indeed has been occurring in labour-intensive industries (e.g. textiles). In this regard the 1992 internal market programme, while certainly serving to intensify competition (and extending it to previously protected sectors such as services) only accentuates a more general trend and problem for high wage cost economies. On the other hand, the fact that the competition is more likely to come from the Republic of Korea, Taiwan, or China, than from within the EC hardly invalidates trade union concerns about 'social dumping'.
>
> (Mosley, 1990: 160–1)

The real problem is likely to be not so much a shift in low wage/low skill production, as its institutionalization in present locations. The losers from a Single European Market pursuing a 'quality' scenario are likely to be those with low wage economies (or a preponderance of such sectors) and unregulated labour markets, so that existing disadvantages and sectoral specializations become institutionalized. That means the UK will continue to compete where its competitive advantage lies – in low wage, labour intensive, low skill, low productivity sectors. Already, British-owned multinationals are heavily-biased towards non-manufacturing (Marginson, 1992) and low technology industries (Stopford and Turner, 1985), with a low level of skills and research activity. In the absence of a specific industrial policy to reverse this trend, this bias is likely to persist.

'EUROPEAN' FIRMS?

While the Single European Market will affect firms of all sizes, the focus in most studies is on large multinationals. These suggest a growing importance for internationally mobile employees, which many commentators interpret as meaning the development of a new breed of 'Euromanager' (Bruce, 1989). Most such studies and commentaries, however, fail to discriminate between the different types of employee the SEM will affect. Atkinson's (1989) analysis is the most effective in this respect, in identifying four principal groups for whom mobility will be a significant issue in the SEM. They are:

- senior managers;
- leading scientific and technical staff ('boffins');
- younger managers on development programmes who could expect to experience international assignments at some time;
- graduate recruits.

Some of the resourcing issues for these specific groups, drawing on Atkinson and other studies, are summarized below.

Senior managers

Most studies identify this group as critical to the success of their businesses, but note that suitably international senior managers are in short supply. A 1986 survey of 440 European firms, for example, reported that a shortage of international managers was hampering expansion abroad (*International Management*, 1986), while more recently Scullion's (1992) study of forty-five British and Irish firms found two-thirds had experienced such shortages, with slightly more anticipating shortages in the future. Atkinson's (1989: 10) study of thirty-five major multinationals operating in the UK, with employees across Europe, confirms this, but notes the numbers involved are very small. Most multinationals count them in tens rather than hundreds, and even the largest numbers only about 200. They are 'numerically insignificant' but 'qualitatively vital'.

An interesting shift has been occurring in how firms acquire this group of managers. In the past, firms have relied on internal development as much as on external recruitment. Most of Atkinson's (1989: 48–51) firms, however, reported increasing reliance on outside recruitment. Among the reasons for this are:

- a shortage of managers with the necessary depth of experience;
- the failure of past ways of organizing and developing this cadre to produce the requisite depth and breadth of experience – specifically, the failure of the expatriate system to move people around sufficiently;

• increasing demand as firms move into new spatial markets.

Recruiting such people is typically beyond the capacity of companies' own personnel function, and many therefore rely on international executive search agencies (or 'headhunters').

Scientific and technical staff

Atkinson's (1989: 51–4) focus here is on the few key people who are world leaders in their field. They are people who are personally known and can be identified by a company's own R&D staff, although active recruitment again is likely to lie with specialist headhunters. It is evident that this group follows the international division of R&D, being attracted by superior resources, job challenge, and the proximity of an academic scientific research milieu. The attraction of a warm climate to work in, such as that of California or the south of France, also ranks high, except in biochemistry and pharmaceuticals – sectors where the UK retains leadership.

Younger managers on development programmes

Atkinson (1989: 54–8) identifies significant changes in internal management development systems in relation to this group. These changes reflect the dissatisfaction with the old expatriate system and the new demands on senior managers. In effect, large multinationals are trying to create a more flexible and enlarged internal labour market of young, internationally experienced managers to overcome the deficiences now being experienced in the supply of suitably qualified senior executives. The emphasis on early, shorter, and frequent assignments for more up-and-coming managers corresponds to the shifts in practice referred to earlier at BP and Shell. Large Continental European companies like Olivetti, Rhône-Poulenc, Accor, Hoechst and Fiat are also prominent in developing programmes to recruit and develop young Euro-managers (Barham and Oates, 1991: 124–31).

Graduate recruits

Nothing in relation to the above groups in Atkinson is specific to the European scene, however. As he notes, this is precisely because the multinationals concerned do not regard the European market as uniquely important – for the largest companies, the USA and Pacific rim are, if anything, more so. Europe figures more, however, in graduate recruitment. Consequently, the development of a single European labour market is likely to be of most immediate significance in relation to graduates. As the feedstock to management development programmes and scientific/technical activity, graduate recruitment has therefore attracted particular interest.

Atkinson's (1989: 58–60) multinationals gave two reasons for being interested in recruiting on the European continent:

1 to overcome the impending demographic downturn in the UK's graduate supply, particularly of scientific and technical graduates;
2 to increase the overall quality of graduate intake, not necessarily in individual terms, but in the variety of people from different backgrounds entering the general management stream.

A limited pool of suitably qualified talent throughout Europe means, for example, that British-based companies are vulnerable because (i) Britain turns out, at its highest level, educated young managers who are more willing than most to move abroad early in their career (Bruce, 1989), (ii) English is the language of international business, and so the British are attractive recruits, and (iii) managerial salaries in the UK are still lower than on the Continent (Bruce, 1989; Scullion, 1992).

A study by ACOST (the UK Advisory Council on Science and Technology) supports this view, citing the fact that graduates in Britain are usually younger (because courses are shorter and they do not have to do national service), and are more willing to travel. ACOST therefore expects a net loss of young scientists. The Department of Education and Science, however, is reported to have rejected this view, believing that EC-wide acceptance of professional qualifications will make degree courses in the UK attractive to Continental students (*The Higher*, 1991a) – by implication, thereby increasing the supply available in Britain.

In the short-term, however, the prospect of continued and growing shortages of internationally experienced managers and of graduates is encouraging companies to look beyond their national boundaries. At first sight, this might seem to be self-defeating if all companies are chasing a limited pool, especially as the demographic downturn implies fewer young people coming onto the European labour market. However, those companies that can gain a march in attracting good graduates will be at a long-term advantage. On the other hand, the supply of 'Euro-managers' can be expanded if many companies simply take graduates and give them training and experience in working on a pan-European scale early on.

All companies, nevertheless, face problems in going outside their own country to recruit (Atkinson, 1989; Barham and Oates, 1991; Scullion, 1992). Problems in recruiting abroad are numerous and present a considerable challenge to the HRM function. They include:

- lack of knowledge of local labour markets;
- lack of a presence in the other country which makes it harder to attract good candidates;
- ignorance of the local education system and the status of qualifications;
- variability in the experience and qualifications of graduates, given the different structures of national systems (for example, German students graduate in their late twenties);
- trying to transfer native recruitment methods to other countries where different systems may apply;
- language and other cultural problems at interviews;
- pay differences and expectations about pay;
- lack of pension portability (less an issue when recruiting graduates);
- constraints on and attitudes to mobility.

There are, for instance, fundamental differences between the UK and many other European countries in recruiting graduates (Keenan, 1991). Other countries rely much more on graduates making direct application to firms, and do not operate the equivalent of our 'milk-round', whereby companies present themselves on campuses with the active support of career services in the universities. On the Contintent, direct applications are encouraged by company links with academics and through work placements. This system exists also in the UK, of course, through sandwich courses and for specialist technical subjects. Indeed, the milk-round, which is expensive, labour-intensive, and increasingly ineffective in picking up the best talent, is falling somewhat out of favour in the UK. Whether the UK system is becoming more like the Continental system or not, recruiting in Europe means a greater role for personal contacts, making it harder for a firm without a very strong presence already in the other country to attract graduate recruits.

Differences of this kind are beginning to be more thoroughly documented. The IPM in conjunction with Income Data Services publishes a guide on recruitment practices in European countries, while the Price Waterhouse/Cranfield (1990) project aims to document aspects of human resource management in recruitment, pay and benefits, training and development, employee relations, and employment practices in companies across the EC and non-EC European countries over a five-year period. The IPM also has a study on graduate recruitment which reports at the end of 1992.

EC initiatives to develop comparability in qualifications, promote language development, and encourage student mobility are beginning to ease other difficulties and pave the way towards a common graduate labour market, through ERASMUS, TEMPUS and, in FE and youth training, PETRA. ERASMUS, for instance, was launched in 1987 to encourage student exchanges and language development, and through exchanges of academic staff encourage the development of compatible teaching programmes. So far, it has succeeded in involving only 2–3 per cent of the student population, instead of the projected 10 per cent by 1992/93, because of budget limitations on the grants available (*The Higher*, 1991b). Within this scheme, the UK is a net importer of students, and also has difficulty apparently in attracting science and engineering students – the suggestion being that this is due to science students dropping language studies to undertake the narrower A-level curriculum in the UK. This may begin to change with the extension of language teaching on specialist degree courses in most universities now (*The Higher*, 1991c).

Whether this improvement in the supply of graduates with a European outlook benefits British firms, however, depends on British firms themselves. Keenan's (1991) survey of 127 large UK and sixty-two broadly equivalent French companies, for instance, shows the French much more active in EC recruitment outside their own borders – 45 per cent, compared with less than 20 per cent of UK firms, recruiting graduates in significant numbers. Among those not yet recruiting, moreover, 60 per cent of French but only 25 per cent of British firms had plans to do so. This tallies with other evidence that the French are taking to the concept of the Single European Market more wholeheartedly, as an expression of national pride and from a sense of national destiny (Barsoux and Lawrence, 1991: 207–8).

Keenan also found the French firms were much more positive about the need for graduates to have a knowledge of European cultures, to obtain part of their education in another European country, and to gain experience of working abroad. Interestingly, more of the British firms claimed to be making changes to their graduate training, although these were a minority and the changes were often relatively minor.

Keenan suggests three initiatives to remedy the deficiencies of British firms. First, they need to review their selection criteria to identify those additional qualities graduates will need to operate effectively in a European context. Second, recruiters will need to know where such graduates can best be found, which may mean having a knowledge of the relevant educational systems. And, third, they should target those institutions which have taken up the European challenge in modifying existing courses and introducing European degrees.

An important issue for HRM in all this is the need to see these kinds of labour market issues in terms not just of demand. Companies have an implicit sense of this when they identify problems of retention alongside recruitment and training difficulties (for example, in Wood and Peccei, 1990). More often, however, when they articulate recruitment issues arising from internationalization or the SEM, they see themselves as the prime or sole actor. As Atkinson notes (1989: 44), 'insofar as they have thought about it at all, our respondents tended to see the question of internationalization of the workforce largely as a demand side issue in which they are the key agent, and the workforce is passive'.

On the contrary, in a situation of European labour shortages for highly qualified personnel, UK companies are inevitably in competition with European companies, whether on the Continent or in the UK. As a result, the intentions of UK firms are only part of the demand equation. They are already part of an international market, competing for certain kinds of skill and employee, and this tendency will increase. Thus, in making their plans for employment and developing human resource strategies for getting and keeping employees, UK firms will have to take into account the plans of companies elsewhere in Europe (and those of incoming Japanese and American firms) more than they are doing. This is yet another instance of seeing the domestic market in international terms.

The issue of recruitment also reinforces a second general theme developed in Chapter 2 about the advantages to international activity of gaining an initial toehold in overseas markets and the virtue of incremental expansion. What is true of business development is true of HRM. Being present in European (and other) markets helps firms to understand and solve the human resource problems that accompany business expansion in anticipation of larger commitments.

Thus, the study by Wood and Peccei (1990) on British firms' preparedness for 1992 shows that the biggest influence on firms developing human resource policies for Europe is the nature of their current involvement. If they sell into the EC or have employees elsewhere in the EC already, they are far more likely to have a European dimension to their HRM than if they have no presence. As an illustration of this, those firms which are most active in monitoring pay and benefits and researching the comparability of professional and vocational qualifications are ones which are already involved in Europe, irrespective of any present plans to recruit in the EC (Wood and Peccei, 1990).

Other employees: a European labour market?

These four groups aside, Atkinson (1989) neverthless notes that even in major multinationals the vast majority of employees are unlikely to be internationally mobile. Local conditions of employment will remain the norm for most people for the foreseeable future until the EC makes real progress in harmonizing standards. Wood and Peccei's (1990: 68–71) survey reinforces this impression, in that the development of common EC practices on employment is well down the list of firms' concerns.

This is not to say there are not important ways in which the majority of the workforce do need to adapt their attitudes and skills for internationalization. While the firms in Wood and Peccei's (1990) study are most concerned with developments affecting managerial employees, they also perceive general implications for secretarial and clerical employees as much as for engineers and technicians beyond the question of mobility.

Notwithstanding scepticism about the likely extent of employee mobility, the European Commission continues to develop comparability in vocational standards and mutual recognition of qualifications to facilitate a European labour market. Underlying this is the same motivation and perspective which animates the removal of trade barriers – the belief that economic growth is restricted by the inefficient allocation of resources. Common systems for accrediting skills will enable scarce skills to be spread more efficiently across the Community.

Systematic data on imbalances at a sectoral level are not available, although Rajan (1990: 109) suggests recent economic recessions have led to people being employed at a level below their education and qualifications, and this has tied up skills that could be put to better use elsewhere. Projections for graduate supply, however, do suggest that, at present levels of output, some member countries (Germany) will develop surpluses, while others (France) will experience shortages. Potential shortages in France may explain the keen interest in graduate recruitment exhibited in Keenan's (1991) study. (However, since the UK is also forecast to experience a dearth of graduates (IMS, 1989) this factor cannot account for UK employers' relative indifference.)

The European Commission has so far adopted agreements on mutual recognition of qualifications in six medical professions and on trades in six other industries (hotel and catering, motor vehicle repairs, construction, electrical engineering, agriculture/ horticulture/forestry, textiles, and clothing). However, actual mobility in these has so far been negligible (Bruce, 1989). Extension of these arrangements is slow, among other reasons, because of the adherence of countries to different ways of assessing and certificating competencies. Italy and Germany, for instance, prefer input-based measures (the achievement of formal qualifications), while the UK has become committed to output-based measures in the form of NVQs which have replaced the older input model associated with apprenticeships. Nor has inter-country exchange of information on vacancies been particularly effective.

The reality, therefore, as Rajan (1990: 111) concludes, is that we are unlikely to see much movement between countries, but rather continued occupational and sectoral mobility within member states. Rainbird sums up the effort to promote a Single European Labour Market, through equivalent vocational qualifications, as follows:

The basic assumptions behind the comparability exercise have been demonstrated as flawed. This is because labour mobility at European level is limited and is unlikely to increase in the absence of qualitative changes in the scale and extent of cultural and linguistic integration envisaged by the Community. In contrast, historical patterns of labour migration suggest that mobility from outside the Community has been and will continue to be more significant in terms of volume. The response of the Community in this instance has been to attempt to restrict mobility.

(Rainbird, 1992: 29)

The actual figures at first sight might appear to contradict this. For example, in 1988, the number of foreign nationals in the UK accounted for 4.5 per cent of the UK labour force, and in the South East amounted to as much as one in eight of the working population (Salt and Kitching, 1990). Among these, the number of workers from EC countries averaged 383,000 between 1984–8, and overall (taking in the peak of the economic cycle) they increased in that period by 10 per cent. A significant number of these were corporate transferees, accounting for around one in five of all foreign nationals in professional and managerial jobs (Salt and Kitching, 1990; *Employment Gazette*, 1991).

However, the great majority of foreign nationals were in lower status manual jobs and represent historic patterns of migration from particular countries. People from southern Ireland, for example, are the biggest single group of all foreign nationals in the UK. They account for 66 per cent of all workers from EC countries, and are typically concentrated in manual jobs in building and construction. Many hotels and restaurants in London and the South East similarly rely on workers from the Continent. Although these occupations are among those on which the EC has concluded mutual recognition agreements, it is doubtful what impact they have actually had. As Salt and Kitching note, the trend for such groups of workers to be mobile is not new. Though it has grown, there has been similar growth in other skill groups. Standard vocational qualifications are in many cases irrelevant in these kinds of manual jobs where employment is characterized by self-employment and employment in small establishments.

Apart from the speed of adoption, there is also a fundamental problem that developing common formal vocational standards across Europe may create a straitjacket that is at odds with technical progress. People need skills that are adaptable to a range of tasks and capable of continuing enhancement from the point of view both of changing technologies within a sector and the need for mobility between sectors. The special circumstances of smaller firms – skills practised in unconventional ways, niche specialization, and innovation among newer firms – in particular may be at odds with output-based measures of vocational competence (Hendry, Jones and Arthur, 1991: 70–1). How one then defines a vocation or occupation and classifies the skills for it is therefore critical.

The German system which in 1988 classified some 332 recognized occupations and tightly regulated the right to work in these is widely admired, not least in the UK. However, is what Grosser (1989: 30) has called the 'occupational and status ghettoes' of Germany the appropriate model? The development of occupational profiles and classification of skills which CEDEFOP (the EC's centre of training expertise) is undertaking on a European basis (Sellin, 1989; Grootings, 1989), alongside similar work in individual countries including Britain, may be at odds with processes of change in technology and work.

CEDEFOP is, in fact, acutely aware of this issue and the need to maintain flexibility in vocational standards and in skills themselves (Retuerto, 1989: 2). However, it sees the solution lying in a broad preliminary education as an offset to subsequent or parallel vocationalism. Thus, 'the best vocational education in today's rapidly changing society is a solid general education both in terms of breadth and quality' (Husen, 1989: 13). The question for the UK is whether the education and training reforms of recent years in fact tend in this direction, or whether they promote a narrow (or worse, an empty) vocationalism for large sections of the population.

Slow progress and uncertainty in such areas as these and in the adoption and implementation of the Social Chapter tends to justify the fact that many firms are adopting a 'wait and see' attitude to the impact of the SEM on their human resource policies (Wood and Peccei, 1990).

At the same time, the European Commission's initiatives to promote greater mobility and efficiency in the labour market may end up institutionalizing existing disparities between weaker and stronger economies. While there are supply-demand imbalances between trained people and jobs, those, like the UK, with the highest stock of graduates and higher levels of unemployment are vulnerable to losing their most educated workers to those countries which face shortages (as France, for example, does in respect of electronics engineers and computer scientists (Directorate-General for Employment, Industrial Relations and Social Affairs, 1990: 50)).

EUROPEAN HUMAN RESOURCE MANAGEMENT?

In Chapter 4, we considered the competing influences of corporate and national culture on international firms. Institutional structures rooted in history, political and economic systems, and systems of religious beliefs combine together to make one country often very different from another.

The Single European Market is, in many respects, directed at the minimization of national differences. At one level, the harmonization of standards across many kinds of product is often perceived, rightly or wrongly, as undermining the distinctiveness of national cultures. At a second level, in seeking to establish basic common rights for employees across all twelve member states, the Social Chapter challenges fundamental differences in the status of the citizen at work and the legal systems which enforce these. Finally, the creation of common, centralized political structures and unified Community institutions for managing financial and economic affairs tends, as the British government well recognizes, towards the convergence of political systems.

Beyond the specific influence of the Single European Market, the increasing internationalization of business promotes the spread of management ideas and practices across national boundaries. During this century, convergence has been fuelled by the world-wide export particularly of American management practice (Hendry, 1991). 'Scientific management' has undoubtedly been the most successful such practice. Other practices, such as Management by Objectives, quality circles, divisionalized organization structures, and strategic planning have had a more variable impact. More recently, of course, Western countries have tried to adopt elements of the Japanese management system.

Underlying the export of ideas and management methods, contingency theorists from Kerr et al. (1960) onwards argue that world-wide economic trends and the transfer of technology produce pressures for convergence which translate into similar patterns of adjustment at the organizational level.

The balance between the forces of diversity and homogenization determines, at the individual level, the adjustment which managers and others need to make in international firms. At the institutional and collective level, national differences affect the extent to which personnel management in different countries develops along common or similar lines. This then affects the ability of a company to apply common standards and practices in its human resource management to give all international employees a common frame of reference, or, by contrast, how far its HRM needs to be responsive to national differences. Corporately, the issues of national similarity and difference affect the success or failure of mergers, acquisitions, and alliances.

Internationalization in general and the SEM in particular is an encouragement to be clearer about what is distinctive and intractable, as well as best practice, in the different member states. National differences may matter more, not less (Krulis-Randa, 1991). Internationalization and the SEM have paradoxically therefore provided a stimulus to the comparative study of national systems of HRM and personnel management (Pieper, 1990; Brewster and Tyson, 1991), industrial relations (Baglioni and Crouch, 1990; Hyman and Ferner, 1992), and business cultures (Randlesome *et al.*, 1990) within Europe.

There are a great many themes of relevance to such comparative studies. Barsoux and Lawrence (1991) identify a number of such themes concerned with cultural differences:

1 Different views and philosophies of business – these are expressed, for instance, in attitudes to profit and returns to stakeholders, in the culture relating to acquisitions and mergers, in the financial structures which underpin these, and in the relations between business and the State.
2 Management style – including the respect accorded the practical versus the theoretical, the attachment to planning versus pragmatism, and the role of personalities and figureheads in company affairs and in expressing national values.
3 Systems and attitudes relating to industrial democracy.
4 Perspectives on the international scene, regional affiliations and orientations (for example, Germany's towards central and Eastern Europe, Spain's towards South America, and Britain's

towards North America and the British Commonwealth and the idea of free trade).

5 How different countries in Europe, as a result, view the Single European Market within broader processes of internationalization.

6 The 'mental maps' managers bring to their understanding of markets and strategic options.

In addition, we may add a number of interlinked themes specific to HRM:

7 National systems for education and training, with the values that underlie these.

8 The way in which national labour markets work, and particularly the way in which external labour markets interact with internal labour markets.

9 Differential practices and cultural values in relation to specific HRM practices such as job descriptions, appraisal, promotion, and pay.

10 Nationally-specific models of personnel management and HRM embracing all these.

This is a considerable agenda and we will merely review a handful of these. It is worth noting, however, that European mergers and acquisitions will have to negotiate the whole range of these if the process of rationalization within the EC is to be successful.

'Mental maps': learning in internationalization

The idea of managers' 'mental maps' is itself a fascinating mix of many influences. These range from the detailed knowledge of national markets and the consumer tastes and habits which underlie these; through assumptions about mission and commitment to product characteristics in which may be embedded a nation's view of itself (for example, the German commitment to product quality); to patterns of industry structure which condition perceived strategic options. Such 'maps' or 'paradigms' can be specific to industries, countries, or to both. The difficulty with such maps, both for those holding them and those of other nations, is that they are made up of various taken-for-granted understandings, and are therefore to some degree impenetrable (Johnson, 1987). The ability to change oneself or to innovate in another's market lies then with those who can come to terms with what is taken for granted:

> Bringing together these mental maps then, can be a contribution to the understanding of a developing Europe and also the generation of strategic options. However, most firms in our survey are not seeking to achieve such cross-fertilisation. They are attempting to deal with Europe in terms of their historically formed view of the world. Arguably the countries that will succeed in Europe will be those that can break away from such constraints. But is this possible?
>
> (Atamer and Johnson, 1991: 228)

However, as Robert Locke (1991) reminds us elsewhere, taken-for-granted understandings about markets (the 'mental maps' managers bring to strategic decisions) are largely locked up in the subtleties of national language. The fact that English has become the international language of business is a disadvantage in this respect because it gives others greater potential access in understanding English markets than the English have of non-English markets.

The theme of managers' 'mental maps' therefore raises the question of adaptability (or learning) in internationalization. We have already touched on this elsewhere in the analogous situation of 'inter-cultural competence' described in Chapter 4. The remedies on offer are also similar. At one level, there is a developing body of literature on European business cultures which simply aims to impart information (for example, Randlesome et al., 1990). This is rather like briefing the manager about to go on an overseas assignment: it informs, but superficially. Nevertheless, a greater focus on the institutional structures in which behaviour, culture, and systems (like HRM) are embedded is very necessary (Hendry and Pettigrew, 1990). This has often been lacking in studies of management culture where attitudinal and perceptual factors have tended to predominate as a result of using survey techniques, or where the aim has simply been to extract lessons for best practice (Cool and Lengnick-Hall, 1985). Ultimately, though, competence requires total immersion, in language and culture.

Employment systems

During the 1980s, there has been increasing interest in documenting the achievements of different systems of education and training within Europe and elsewhere, given the relative performance of the UK as an industrial nation (Hayes, Anderson and Fonda, 1984; Handy, 1987; Prais and Wagner, 1988; Wagner, 1991). As part of this, there is increasing recognition of the economic and institutional factors that underpin and shape such differences (for example, Warner, 1987, 1991; Dore and Sako, 1989; Lane, 1990). This appreciation is enriched by the growing literature on the educational, training, cultural, and status characteristics of occupations in different countries, including managers (for example, Lawrence, 1980; Smith, 1990; Thurley, 1991).

An historical view of the origins of these institutional characteristics is especially valuable as it may also reveal the potential for change. Takahashi's (1990) account of the Japanese employment system is a good example of this, showing in the process both the relatively recent origins of much that is taken for granted in the Japanese system, and the areas of strain in the present system. The origins of occupational definitions and training in Germany within the ancient guild system is a similar case.

A full appreciation of how employment systems work and are formed must also take account of the way organizations interact with the external labour market for different occupations and help to construct occupational profiles, definitions, and competences. As Windolf (1986) noted some years ago, the impact of firms' recruitment and selection practices in this respect has been much neglected.

These kind of issues ought to be central to personnel management and HRM (Hendry, 1994), but so far have not been. Industrial relations theory, in contrast, has been concerned with employment systems, their origins, how they work, how they are sustained, and how they change, but has tended to come at these issues in a rather partial and often tangential way, focused on the role of trade unions.

An illustration of the more direct approach that is needed is provided by Eyraud, Marsden and Silvestre (1990), who analyse occupational and internal labour markets for skilled manufacturing workers in Britain and France. They argue, for instance, that training practices, labour market structure, industrial relations systems and patterns of labour management combine to produce quite different labour markets in the two countries – an occupational model predominating in the UK, an internal labour market model predominating in France. In the same way, it is impossible to understand German firms without appreciating their elaborate internal labour markets, brought about by high barriers against temporary lay-offs and the extensive (government-sponsored) involvement of works councils in decisions on the level of employment (Wachter and Stengelhofen, 1992). If this structure were to erode, the much-admired national system of training might itself begin to unravel.

Although less bound up in legislative structures, managerial labour markets are no less conditioned by cultural and institutional factors – as the modelling of management development systems by Evans, Lank and Farquhar (1989) and Evans (1990), described in Chapter 4, illustrates.

This kind of understanding of labour markets and how they work is important to any company operating in different countries, especially where, in the case of elite groups like managers, it may inadvertently impose a culturally specific internal labour market model that does not tally with the way the external labour market works.

Human resource systems and practices

At a more mundane level we are only just beginning to appreciate the extent of national differences in Europe across a wide range of personnel practices. The Price Waterhouse/Cranfield Project will contribute a great deal to our knowledge of trends here. Published papers so far cover flexible patterns of work (Brewster *et al.*, 1992), and equal opportunities (Hegewisch, 1992). However, reported differences in particular areas of HRM and personnel management between European countries need to be sensitive to the meanings people in different countries attribute to specific practices (Hendry, 1991). In other words, one needs to understand the cultural milieu in which particular practices are located.

For companies, this is important when they try to transfer employment practices from one location to another. As Cappelli and McKiersie (1987) note, effective transfer requires a 'platform' where the lessons for transferring change can be learnt, which implies some basis of commonality in the culture that new human resource practices can fit into. In other words, what we have here is a problem of organizational learning, analogous to that involved in strategic alliances, which has to take in knowledge that is tacit and taken-for-granted.

With this in mind, Rogot (1990) discusses some of the problems involved in the transfer of Anglo-Saxon management culture to France, including resistance to management by objectives (Trepo, 1975) and quality circles (Arnoux and Hermel, 1985), while Schneider (1988) draws attention to a wide range of mismatches which occur when multinationals try to transfer human resource practices. Significant differences can thus be found in company practices and employee attitudes within different countries towards:

- the definition of skills and job descriptions;
- selection and promotion criteria;
- geographic mobility (including the readiness to accept international assignments);
- performance measurement and appraisal (including MBO and societal attitudes to face-to-face feedback);
- performance-based pay;
- pay differentials, and the trade-off between money, status, and leisure;
- personal autonomy versus corporate socialization.

When considering specific differences like these within their cultural context, it is also helpful to keep in view the general models of personnel and human resource management that exist in different countries. These give expression to national sentiments and values, and provide an integrating framework to isolated employment practices. There is a small but growing literature on the characteristics of, and contrasts between, different human resource systems in Europe (for example, Pieper, 1990; Lawrence, 1991; and the twenty-fifth anniversary edition of *Employee Relations*), although much of this is still insufficiently empirical.

One of the key issues such writings address is the extent of convergence that is taking place between national systems, and specifically the scope for an international model of HRM. Although originally an American import (Hendry and Pettigrew, 1990), the concept of 'human resource management' has increasing international currency, and thus focuses the issue of convergence. Is there one model of HRM, or many responding to culturally-specific ways of doing things buttressed by national institutions and value systems? In Germany, for example, there has been considerably less enthusiasm for HRM than in Britain and

France, and there is as yet no formal translation of the term (Wachter and Stengelhofen, 1992).

Part of the problem in assessing convergence is having an agreed yardstick as to what HRM comprises. It will be apparent that we have used the term in this book in only the very loosest sense to refer to activities and processes involving people. In order to assess the degree of convergence towards a common model, however, a tighter definition is needed. One attempt to develop systematic European comparisons, using the integration of HRM issues to business strategy and the devolvement of HRM practices and responsibilities to line management as the key criteria, finds considerable variability across Europe (Brewster and Larsen, 1992). Brewster and Larsen note, however, that the model of high integration and high devolvement which is supposed to characterize HRM (and is most evident in Sweden and Switzerland, and to a lesser extent in Norway and Denmark) is in fact rare even in the USA.

While EC laws and regulations may hasten such a convergence, the most powerful engine for convergence to date has been the multinational company. The best-documented instances of this so far relate to American multinationals in the UK (Cappelli and McElrath, 1992). In the 1960s, American firms were at the forefront of innovations in British industrial relations, such as productivity bargaining, fixed-term agreements, and wage reforms (although these and other innovations, such as company-level bargaining, also occasioned conflicts). Bearing in mind the earlier criticism that multinationals exploit the countries they settle in and lower employment standards ('the new international division of labour'), it is ironic then that multinationals have also been criticized for failing to transfer superior practices from the home country (Capelli and McElrath, 1992). In part, this reflects how ethnocentric or polycentric they are (Perlmutter, 1969), and whether they exercise control over subsidiaries through written policies or the transfer of personnel.

Towards a European model of HRM

While American-inspired HRM has dominated thinking in the UK since the mid-1980s, it may be that as we gain increasing exposure to Continental European systems and EC regulations take effect, a distinctly European model will evolve. Thurley (1990) has suggested four principles which stand out as likely 'building blocks' for a European model of personnel management. These are:

1 the need to provide for dialogue between the 'social partners' at all levels;
2 the need to build organizations on a multi-cultural basis to preserve different ways of thinking and behaving and allow expression of different cultural identities;
3 the need for a democratic form of enterprise;
4 the need to provide for continuous learning by staff and objective evaluation of results on a scientific basis – 'The European enterprise is likely to have a strong intellectual tradition and to value critical debate' (Thurley, 1990).

Shell, Olivetti, and Siemens are said to display some of these principles already. The IDS/IPM (1988) report on personnel management and the Single European Market provides other examples of how individual companies have accommodated national idiosyncracies to the need for coordinated and compatible policies across the organization.

In conclusion, then, just as personnel management in the past has reflected tensions and accommodations within industrial British society, so is a European model of personnel management likely to have to do so on a European scale:

> The fundamental issue posed by European integration in the end comes down to the question of what type of society is being proposed. In this sense, personnel management must become one of a number of critical political issues.
>
> (Thurley, 1990: 57)

CONCLUSION

This chapter has covered a wide range of issues associated with three themes. First, there is the question of how the Single European Market will affect employment and what member states will need to do to achieve the economic benefits. The main thrust of EC policy is the development of high skill economies and firms, while encouraging the efficient use of scarce skills across the Community.

Second, processes of rationalization and concentration among companies are expected to lead to the formation of 'European' firms. This will mean increased mobility of key employee groups within companies. If genuine European firms are to form, they will need to operate on a polycentric basis, rather than through the imposition of a single national identity. In the short term, however, it may be more reasonable to expect the acquisition process to have an aggressive nationalistic character. On the other hand, acquisitions that are undertaken in this way may be more likely to unravel or fail commercially. It may be better therefore to go into acquisitions and mergers from the beginning intending to create multiple centres of influence and draw different nationalities into key positions.

Third, this raises the question of how far or soon we may see the evolution of a European model of HRM. This exposes national differences rooted in institutions and culture, as well as the potential of international firms to spread best practice in technology and HRM. We are just beginning to appreciate these differences. From this point of view, the SEM has already had one extremely positive effect in making us more aware of superior employment practices elsewhere in Europe.

The aim of the Single European Market is to turn an international market (the EC) into something more like a domestic one. As in the case of internationalization generally, this means becoming more aware of both sameness and difference. While the European Commission encourages harmonization in various areas, including employment, this will only be successful if we fully appreciate the cultural, social, psychological differences that underlie regulatory structures. HRM operates at both these levels in the company and institutionally.

Chapter 7

Concluding comments
HRM and the 1990s

TRENDS IN THE INTERNATIONAL ECONOMY

According to Buckley (1991), several important trends seem likely to influence the world economy throughout the 1990s:

- an increase in both competition and collaboration between firms;
- political changes, including deregulation, especially the fall-out from the dissolution of the former command economies of Russia and East Europe, and the process of integration in Western Europe;
- the continuing impact of technological imperatives;
- social changes involving life-styles and 'green' issues;
- the restructuring of the world economy arising from the impact of all the above, at a number of levels, from the national to the firm to relations between firms.

In the 1980s, the imperatives of competition revolved around, first, new standards for quality, cost, cycle time, responsiveness to customers, and flexibility, and second, beginning to learn how to balance the demands of global products and local responsiveness. In the 1990s, managers will be confronted with an additional set of demands arising from the way competition is conducted (Prahalad, 1990). On top of the general trends outlined above, these represent a considerable increase in complexity. They include:

- shifting patterns of trade and funds flow across the regions of the world, so that managers will have to think in terms of trading blocs and economic regions rather than nation states;

- the restructuring of mature industries, with governments taking a keen interest in this through the overall impacts on smaller firms and levels of competition in the national economy;
- competition to establish standards in emerging industries, with the implications this has for securing market dominance;
- managing collaborations;
- competing for core competencies related to the understanding of emerging new products and markets, so that firms retain vitality through their capacity to create new businesses;
- related to this, being able to secure, retain, and protect the intellectual property embedded in people, which is more difficult than simply protecting manufacturing processes and traditional products through patents;
- understanding the importance of blending hardware and software in products and services (a definition that erodes in the process), and how to put the relevant skills together in businesses;
- coping with transformations in the basic paradigms and the disciplines behind these in many industries, with the changes in the skill and knowledge base this entails.

Two things stand out in this list. First, there is the way competition is increasingly based in people-related 'invisible assets' (Teece, 1987). Human resource strategies are therefore likely to assume a more central role in business growth strategies. Second, many of these trends are not exclusive to internationalization, in the sense of trading abroad. What internationalization does is to accelerate and widen the competitive arena, unsettling the basis of competition for domestically oriented and internationalized firms alike. This is simply the process of ever-widening markets, exacerbated at the present time by advancing technology. This has been a central theme throughout this book:

> In certain respects, global management is no different from domestic management in the competitive issues that need to be addressed, while internationalization is simply the process of leveraging domestic core competencies and transferring competitive advantages.

The challenge of internationalization is how exactly this is done.

A FUTURE OF GLOBAL TRANSNATIONAL FIRMS?

There are, however, major differences of opinion as to how internationalized the world economy already is or will become. This applies to both the 'concentration of economic activity' thesis and the 'transnationalization' argument which sees international firms dispersing activities around the globe.

On the concentration issue, there are those like Bower (1988) who see the world economy falling under the sway of five or six major players in sector after sector, amid the creation of worldwide oligopolies. Many major industries in the USA have already rationalized down to a handful of firms in the face of Japanese competition, and Bower sees Europe succumbing to the same process, with the dominant oligopolies that eventually emerge being mainly Japanese. The scope for rationalization in the EC is evident from comparisons with the USA. At the last count, the EC had fifty tractor manufacturers, the USA had four; the EC had 300 domestic appliance manufacturers, the USA had four; the EC had eleven manufacturers of railway stock, the USA had two; the EC had eleven manufacturers of telephone exchanges, the USA had four; and so on (Rajan, 1990). The Single European Market is clearly designed to encourage a process of rationalization.

Allied to the 'concentration' or 'globalization' thesis is the 'transnational' argument that success will fall to those organizations that can successfully coordinate their activity across borders and exploit their international networks, so that they utilize technology developed in one place, to meet market demand in another, through production in possibly a third location (Porter, 1986; Bartlett and Ghoshal, 1989; Spivey and Thomas, 1990; and Dicken, 1992).

In contrast to these scenarios, there is the evidence of how technological activity is actually concentrated. The focus on technological innovation is important, first, because the competitive game ultimately rests upon technological progress, and second, because the organizational challenge of capturing synergies across borders is largely determined by the extent to which technology is dispersed outside the country in which the firm is headquartered.

Using evidence from patents granted in the USA from 1969–86, Pavitt and Patel (1990) reject both theses of 'globalization' and the 'transnational'. First, large firms account for around 60 per cent of the world's technological activities undertaken by firms – or, alternatively, firms with less than 8,000 employees still account for 40 per cent. Although these figures might in some eyes suggest that large firms are dominant, they are biased by the relative importance of large firms in a few sectors, notably the chemicals, motor vehicles, and electrical/electronic sectors.

Second, Pavitt and Patel find that less than 20 per cent of the technological activity of large firms in the eleven most advanced industrialized countries is performed abroad, with the exception of the Netherlands and Switzerland. They therefore conclude that:

> the production of technology remains highly 'domesticated' in two senses. First, in most of the countries at the world's technological frontier, the foreign technological activities of large firms are still not the major feature. Second, large firms' technological performance is strongly dependent on the performance of the home country.
>
> (Pavitt and Patel, 1990: 24)

This is in line with Porter's (1990) more recent work which suggests that home countries still matter greatly. Pavitt and Patel go on to argue that:

> country-specific factors create both the general conditions that determine the volume of technological activities, and the specific inducement mechanisms that determine their direction [that is, the particular sectors in which countries and the firms therein are successful and specialise].
>
> (Pavitt and Patel, 1990: 24)

Interestingly, the exception is the USA, which has a number of large firms that are strong abroad in sectors of relative domestic weakness. This suggests that the transnational model may be distinctively American. However, if all sectors are taken into account, US firms tend to locate less technological activity abroad than firms of other industrialized countries (Cantwell, 1990). Other countries than the USA may in fact be better candidates for the transnational model because of small domestic markets (Netherlands and Switzerland), and/or for political reasons to get inside the tarrif walls of important trading blocs (Sweden). For political reasons similarly, Japanese firms may start to go down the transnational route.

The general implications of Pavitt and Patel's data, however, is for a model of the firm which falls short of Bartlett and Ghoshal's more adventurous prescriptions. Because national systems of education, training, and basic research therefore remain critical, and because the links between these are 'person-embodied',

> it may well be more efficient to have technological activities nationally concentrated, with international 'listening posts' and adaptive capabilities maintained through small foreign laboratories, frequent international exchanges often involving what are called 'strategic alliances', and proximity to an internationally outward looking system of higher education.
>
> (Pavitt and Patel, 1990: 25)

This is important because it puts the emphasis on domestic human resource strengths and organizational flexibility focused on alliances, with relatively little interchange between dispersed R&D activities within the firm. This is not to say that production and sales may not be dispersed in many locations and require coordinating, but these do not require such complex flows of information and people.

However, there is some disagreement about the location of technological innovation in respect to the UK. Although supporting Pavitt and Patel's general conclusions about the relative importance of domestic versus foreign-based technological activity, Cantwell (1990) produces a diametrically opposite conclusion regarding the UK, despite drawing ostensibly on the same data-set over the same timescale (1969–86).

Thus, according to Cantwell, British firms are relatively heavily dependent upon foreign research facilities (certainly when compared with the USA, Japan, Germany, France, and Italy), and have been at the forefront of the internationalization of research activity (along with the Netherlands, Belgium, and Switzerland). They are especially reliant on overseas technological activity in coal and petroleum products, mechanical engineering, food products, mineral products and metals (reflecting sectors which have a strong imperial tradition), and are increasingly so in textiles and motor vehicles. At the same time, the UK has become less important as a technological centre for foreign firms in a range of sectors, including electrical equipment, motor vehicles, aircraft and textiles.

These trends are compatible with the general decline in UK industrial performance (reflected in the analysis in Chapters 5 and 6), and in line with the view that foreign inward investment in the

UK has been in 'screwdriver' plants, rather than in enhancing the technological base.

The significance of this lies in differing requirements for skills and mobility among different groups of employees. A net export of R&D activity means more scientific and technical workers going abroad (the 'brain drain'), while an inward flow of capital investment on production facilities is likely to draw in foreign production managers, with two-way exchanges possibly from the UK. In other words, patterns of inward and outward investment have different effects on the requirements for human resources in the aggregate and on what HRM in the firm has to manage.

HRM: A PROCESSUAL VIEW

The forms of international business have become increasingly complex. In this book we have analysed the human resource issues that arise in exporting, alliances, and within the multinational firm. Within the framework of the Single European Market, we have also looked at the issues involved in mergers and acquisitions as European firms rationalize and join forces. To understand this complexity we have set out relevant theories of internationalization. Even so, the forms of internationalization continue to run ahead of such theories. The recourse to acquisitions is the obvious example of this, since it tends to negate the 'leveraging of domestic competences' argument and transcends 'internalization' theory and the 'eclectic paradigm' which incorporates it.

Reference to such theories may tend to complicate things if one conceives of HRM as simply a set of techniques or activities which help large organizations to manage international managers – which is what much of the international HRM literature amounts to. On the other hand, this literature does little to address the much bigger question of international growth. This book has therefore tried to connect the underlying processes of internationalization to some of the distinctive human resource processes and issues involved. In doing so, we have stressed basic continuities that exist between domestic and international activity. This has enabled us to relate the internationalization experiences of large and small firms, newly internationalizing and mature international firms. The results, we hope, are lessons for the general manager as well as for the HRM function.

References

Abell, D.F. (1980) *Defining the Business: The Starting Point of Strategic Planning*, Englewood Cliffs, NJ: Prentice-Hall.

Adler, N.J. (1986) *International Dimensions of Organizational Behaviour*, Boston, Mass.: Kent Publishers.

—— (1987) 'Do MBAs want International Careers?', *International Journal of Intercultural Relations* 10:277–300.

Adler, N.J. and Jelinek, M. (1986) 'Is "Organization Culture" Culture Bound?', *Human Resource Management* 25(1):73–90.

Adler, N.J., Doktor, R. and Redding, S.G. (1986) 'From the Atlantic to the Pacific Centre: Cross-Cultural Management Reviews', *Journal of Management* 12(2):295–318.

Aharoni, Y. (1966) *The Foreign Investment Decision Process*, Boston, Mass: Graduate School of Business Administration, Harvard University.

Anderson, E. and Gatignon, H. (1986) 'Modes of Foreign Entry: A Transaction Cost Analysis and Propositions', *Journal of International Business Studies* 17(3):1–26.

Arkin, A. (1991) 'How international are Britain's business schools?', *Personnel Management*, November: 28–31.

Arnoux, J.P. and Hermel, P. (1985) 'Cercles de qualité et fonctionnement de l'entreprise: apports limités et effets pervers', *Direction et Gestion* 6.

Atamer, T. and Johnson, G. (1991) 'Conclusions', in R. Calori and P. Lawrence (eds) *The Business of Europe: Managing Change*, London/Newbury Park/New Delhi: Sage.

Atkinson, J. (1989) *Corporate Employment Policies for the Single European Market. IMS Report No. 179*, Institute of Manpower Studies, University of Sussex.

Axelsson, R., Cray, D., Mallory, G.R. and Wilson, D.C. (1991) 'Decision Style in British and Swedish Organizations: A Comparative Examination of Strategic Decision Making', *British Journal of Management* 2:67–79.

Baglioni, G. and Crouch, C. (eds) (1990) *European Industrial Relations: The Challenge of Flexibility*, London/Newbury Park/New Delhi: Sage.

Baliga, C. and Baker, J. (1985) 'Multinational corporate policies for expatriate managers: selection, training, evaluation', *SAM Advanced Management Journal* 50(4):31–8.

Bannock, G. and Albach, H (1991) *Small business policy in Europe, Britain, Germany and the Commission*, London: Anglo-German Foundation.

Bannock and Partners (1990) *Enterprises in the European Community*, Commission of the European Communities, Brussels/Luxembourg.

Barham, K. and Oates, D. (1991) *The International Manager*, London: Economist Books.

Barnett, C.K. (1990) 'The Michigan Global Agenda: Research and teaching in the 1990s', *Human Resource Management* 29(1):5–26.

Barsoux, J-L. and Lawrence, P. (1991) 'Countries, Cultures and Constraints', in R. Calori and P. Lawrence (eds) *The Business of Europe: Managing Change*, London/Newbury Park/New Delhi: Sage.

Bartlett, C.A. and Ghoshal, S. (1989) *Managing Across Borders: The Transnational Solution*, Boston, Mass.: Harvard Business School Press.

Bartlett, C. and Yoshihara, H. (1988) 'New challenges for Japanese multinationals: is organization adaptation their achilles heel?', *Human Resource Management* 27(1):19–43.

Bartlett, C.A., Doz, Y. and Hedlund, G. (eds) (1990) *Managing the Global Firm*, London/New York: Routledge.

Bass, B.M. and Burger, P.C. (1979) *Assessment of Managers: An International Comparison*, New York: Free Press.

Beamish, P.W. and Calof, J.L. (1989) 'International Business Education: A Corporate View', *Journal of International Business Studies* 20(3):553–64.

Becattini, G. (1979) 'Dal settore industriale al distretto industriale', *Rivesto di Economia e Politica Industriale* 1.

Becker, B.M. and Tillman, F.A. (1978) *The Family-Owned Business*, Chicago: Commerce Clearing House.

Begg, I. and Mayes, D. (1991) 'Social and Economic Cohesion Among the Regions of Europe in the 1990s', London: National Institute of Economic and Social Research.

Berney, K. (1990) 'Small Players on the Big Stage', *International Management* April:40–2.

Birley, S. (1985) 'The role of networks in the entrepreneurial process', *Journal of Business Venturing* 1:107–17.

Birley, S., Cromie, S. and Myers, A. (1990) 'Entrepreneurial Networks: Their Emergence in Ireland and Overseas', *International Journal of Small Business* 9(4):56–74.

Bjorkman, I. and Gertsen, M. (1990) 'Corporate expatriation: an analysis of firms and country-specific differences in Scandinavia', unpublished paper.

Black, J. and Mendenhall, M. (1990) 'Cross-cultural training effectiveness: a review and theoretical framework for future research', *Acadamy of Management Review* 15(1):113–36.

Bolton Report (1971) *Report of the Committee of Inquiry on Small Firms*, chaired by J.E. Bolton, Cmnd. 4811, London: HMSO.

Bowen, H.P., De Ghellinck, E., Klepper, G., Lawdy, J., Mayes, D., Pouplier, I., Salvadori, D. and Slenuwaegen, L. (1991) *The European Challenge:*

Response of Industry to the 1992 Programme, Hemel Hempstead: Harvester Wheatsheaf.

Bower, J.L. (1988) *When Markets Quake: The Management Challenge of Restructuring Industry*, Boston: Harvard Business School Press.

Boyce, B. (1992) 'Training and the Single European Market: a case study of the food and drinks processing industries of the UK, France and Germany', 3rd Conference on International Personnel and Human Resources Management, Ashridge Management College, July.

Brewster, C. (1991) *The Management of Expatriates*, London: Kogan Page.

—— and Larsen, H.H. (1992) 'Human resource management in Europe: evidence from ten countries', *International Journal of Human Resource Management* 3(3):409–34.

—— and Tyson, S. (eds) (1991) *International Comparisons in Human Resource Management*, London: Pitman.

——, Hegewisch, A., Lockhart, T. and Mayne, L. (1992) 'Flexible Working Patterns in Europe', Cranfield School of Management.

Bridgewater, S. (1992) 'Informal networks as a vehicle for international market entry: future research directions', *Warwick Business School Research Papers*, No. 54, University of Warwick.

Brislin, R. (1981) *Cross-Cultural Encounters: Face-to-Face Interaction*, New York: Pergamon.

Brooke, M.Z. and Remmers, H.L. (1970) *The Strategy of Multinational Enterprise*, London: Longman.

Bruce, L. (1989) 'Wanted: More Mongrels in the Corporate Kennel', *International Management* January:35–7.

Brusco, S. (1989) 'A policy for industrial districts', in E.Goodman, J. Bamford, and P. Saynor (eds) *Small Firms and Industrial Districts in Italy*, London and New York: Routledge.

Buckley, P.J. (1983) 'New Forms of International Industrial Cooperation: A Survey of the Literature', *Aussenwirtschaft* 38(2):195–222.

—— (1988) 'The Limits of Explanation: Testing the Internalisation Theory of the Multinational Enterprise', *Journal of International Business Studies* XIX(2):181–93.

—— (1991) 'Developments in International Business Theory in the 1990s', *Journal of Marketing Management* 7:15–24.

Buckley, P.J. and Casson, M. (1976) *The Future of the Multinational Enterprise*, London: Macmillan.

—— (1981) 'The Optimal Timing of a Foreign Direct Investment', *Economic Journal* 92(361):75–81.

Buckley, P.J. and Davies, H. (1980) 'Foreign Licensing in Overseas Operations: Theory and Evidence from the UK', in R.G. Hawkins and A.J. Prasad (eds) *Technology Transfer and Economic Development*, Greenwich, Conn.: JAI Press.

Buckley, P.J. and Mathew, A.M. (1979) 'The motivation for recent first-time direct investments in Australia by UK firms', *Management International Review* 19(1):57–69.

Buckley, P.J. and Prescott, K. (1989) 'The Structure of British Industry's Sales in Foreign Markets', *Managerial and Decision Economics* 10(3):189–208.

Buckley, P.J., Newbould, G.D., and Thurwell, J.C. (1988, 2nd edn.) *Foreign Direct Investment by Smaller UK Firms*, London and Basingstoke: Macmillan Press.

Buckley, P.J., Pass, C.L., and Prescott, K. (1990a) 'Foreign Marketing Servicing by Multinationals: An Integrated Treatment', *International Marketing Review* 7(4):25–40.

—— (1990b) 'The Implementation of an International Market Servicing Strategy in UK Manufacturing Firms', *British Journal of Management* 1:127–36.

Buigues, P. and Ilzkovitz, F. (1988) 'The Sectoral Impact of the Internal Market', Commission of the European Communities, DG11, Doc. 11/335/88, Luxembourg.

Business International (1987) 'Competitive Alliances: How to Succeed at Cross-Regional Collaboration', New York: Business International Corporation.

Calori, R. and Lawrence, P. (1991) *The Business of Europe: Managing Change*, London/Newbury Park/New Delhi: Sage.

Cambridge Small Business Research Centre (1992) *The State of British Enterprise*, Small Business Research Centre, University of Cambridge.

Cantwell, J. (1990) 'The Internationalization of Technological Activities and Its Implications for Competitiveness', Economics Department, Reading University.

Cappelli, P. and McElrath, R. (1992) 'The Transfer of Employment Practices Through Multinationals', Center for Human Resources, The Wharton School.

Cappelli, P. and McKiersie, R.B. (1987) 'Management Strategy and the Redesign of Work Rules', *Journal of Management Studies* 24(5):441–62.

Casson, M. (1987) *The Firm and the Market: Studies in Multinational Enterprise and the Scope of the Firm*, London: George Allen & Unwin.

Cecchini, P. (1988) *The European Challenge, 1992: The Benefits of a Single Market*, Aldershot: Wildwood House.

Chandler, A.D. (1962) *Strategy and Structure*, Cambridge, Mass.: MIT Press.

Channon, D.F. (1973) *The Strategy and Structure of British Enterprise*, London: Macmillan.

Church, A. (1982) 'Sojourner Adjustment', *Psychological Bulletin* 91:540–72.

Commission of the European Communities (1985) *Completing the internal market: White Paper from the Commission to the European Council*, Luxembourg.

—— (1988a) *Research on the 'Costs of Non-Europe'*, Luxembourg.

—— (1988b) *The social aspects of the internal market. Vol. 1. Social Europe*, Supplement 7/88, Luxembourg.

—— (1989) *An enterprise policy for the Community* (revised August), Brussels/Luxembourg.

—— (1991) *XXth Report on Competition Policy*, Brussels/Luxembourg.

Conrad, P. and Pieper, R. (1990) 'Human Resource Management in the Federal Republic of Germany', in R. Pieper (ed.) *Human Resource Management: An International Comparison*, Berlin: Walter de Gruyter.

Contractor, F.J. (1980) 'The composition of licensing fees and arrangements as a function of economic development of technology recipient nations', *Journal of International Business Studies* 11(3).

Contractor, F. and Lorange, P. (1988) *Cooperative Strategies in International Business*, Lexington, Mass.: Lexington Books.

Cool, K.O. and Lengnick-Hall, C.J. (1985) 'Some Thoughts on the Transferability of Japanese Management Style', *Organization Studies* 6(1):1–22.

Cooley, M. (1989) *European Competitiveness in the 21st Century: Integration of Work, Culture and Technology*, Brussels: Commission of the European Communities, FAST Programme.

Cowling, K. (1990) 'A New Industrial Strategy: Preparing Europe for the Turn of the Century', *International Journal of Industrial Organization* 8:165–83.

Cowling, K., Stoneman, P., Cubbin, J., Cable, T., Hall, G., Domberger, S., and Dutton, P. (1980) *Mergers and Economic Performance*, Cambridge: Cambridge University Press.

Cummings, L.L., Harnett, D.L. and Stevens, O.J. (1971) 'Risk, Fate, Conciliation, and Trust: An International Study of Attitudinal Differences Among Executives', *Academy of Management Journal*: 285–304.

Curhan, J.P., Davidson, W.H. and Suri, R. (1977) *Tracing the Multinationals: A Sourcebook on US-based Enterprises*, Cambridge, Mass.: Balinger Publishing Co.

Cutler, T., Haslam, C., Williams, J. and Williams, K. (1989) *1992 – The Struggle for Europe: A Critical Evaluation of the European Community*, New York: Berg.

De Cieri, H., Dowling, P.J. and Taylor, K.T. (1991) 'The pyschological impact of expatriate relocation on partners', *International Journal of Human Resource Management* 2(3):377–414.

Derr, C.B. and Oddou, G.R. (1991) 'Are US multinationals adequately preparing future American leaders for global competition', *International Journal of Human Resource Management* 2(2):227–44.

—— (1992) 'Internationalizing Managers: A Report from the Cutting Edge', University of Utah.

Desatnick, R.L. and Bennett, M.L. (1978) *Human Resource Management in the Multinational Company*, New York: Nichols.

Deschampsneuf, H. (1988) *Export for the Small Business*, 2nd edn, London: Kogan Page.

Detweiler, R. (1980) 'Intercultural Interaction and the Categorisation Process: A Conceptual Analysis and Behavioural Outcome', *International Journal of Intercultural Relations* 4:275–93.

Dicken, P. (1992) *Global Shift*, 2nd edn, London: Paul Chapman.

Directorate-General for Economic and Financial Affairs (1988) *European Economy: The Economics of 1992. An assessment of the potential effects of completing the internal market of the European Community*, Brussels: Commission of the European Communities.

—— (1989) *European Economy: Facing the Challenges of the early 1990s*, No. 42, Brussels/Luxembourg: Commission of the European Communities.

—— (1990) *European Economy: Social Europe. The impact of the internal market by industrial sector: the challenge for the Member States*, Brussels: Commission of the European Communities.

Directorate-General for Employment, Industrial and Social Affairs (1990) *Employment in Europe*, Luxembourg: Commission of the European Communities.

—— (1991) *Employment in Europe*, Luxembourg: Commission of the European Communities.

Dore, R.P. and Sako, M. (1989) *How the Japanese Learn to Work*, London: Routledge.

Dowling, P.J. (1988) 'International and Domestic Personnel/Human Resource Management: Similarities and Differences', in R.S. Schuler, S.A. Youngblood and V.L. Huber (eds) *Readings in Personnel and Human Resource Hanagement* (3rd edn), St Paul, Minnesota: West Publishing Co.

Dowling, P.J. and Schuler, R.S (1990) *International Dimensions of Human Resource Management*, Boston, Mass.: PWS-Kent.

Dowling, P.J. and Welch, D. (1988) 'International Human Resource Management: An Australian Perspective', *Asia-Pacific Journal of Management* 6(1): 39–65.

Doz, Y. and Prahalad, C.K. (1986) 'Controlled Variety: A Challenge for Human Resource Management', *Human Resource Management* 25(1):55–71.

Doz, Y., Hamel, G. and Prahalad, C.K. (1986) 'Strategic Partnerships: Success or Surrender?', paper given to conference on 'Cooperative Strategies in International Business', Wharton School/Rutgers University, October.

Doz, Y., Prahalad, C.K. and Hamel, G. (1990) 'Control, change, and flexibility: the dilemma of transnational collaboration', in C.A. Bartlett, Y. Doz, and G. Hedlund (eds) *Managing the Global Firm*, London and New York: Routledge.

Dulfer, E. (1990) 'Human Resource Management in Multinational and Internationally Operating Companies', in R. Pieper (ed.) *Human Resource Management: An International Comparison*, Berlin: Walter de Gruyter.

Dunford, M. and Kafkalar, G. (eds) (1992) *Competition, Regulation and the New Europe*, London: Belhaven.

Dunning, J.H. (1981) *International Production and the Multinational Enterprise*, London: Allen & Unwin.

Dunning, J.H. (1988) 'The Eclectic Paradigm of International Production: A Restatement and Some Possible Extensions', *Journal of International Business Studies* XIX(1).

Dyer, W.G. Jr. (1986) *Cultural Change in Family Firms: Anticipating and Managing Business and Family Transitions*, San Francisco: Jossey-Bass.

Elson, D. (1988) 'Transnational corporations in the new international division of labour: a critique of "cheap labour" hypotheses', Manchester papers on Development, IV:352–76.

Emerson, M., Aujean, M., Catinat, M., Goybet, P. and Jacquemin, A. (1988) *The Economics of 1992: The EC Commission's Assessment of the Economic Effects of Completing the Internal Market*, Oxford: Oxford University Press.

Employment Gazette (1991) 'Foreign workers and the UK labour market: A correction', July:405–8.

Esland, G. (ed.) (1990) *Education, Training and Employment, Volume 1: Educated Labour – The Changing Basis of Industrial Demand*, Reading, Mass.: Addison-Wesley.

Evans, P. (1990) 'International Management Development and the Balance between Generalism and Professionalism', *Personnel Management* December:46–50.

Evans, P. and Lorange, P. (1989) 'The Two Logics Behind Human Resource Management', in P. Evans, Y. Doz and A. Laurent (eds), *Human Resource Management in International Firms*, London: Macmillan.

Evans, P., Doz, Y. and Laurent, A. (1989) *Human Resource Management in International Firms*, London: Macmillan.

Evans, P., Lank, E. and Farquhar, A. (1989) 'Managing Human Resources in the International Firm: Lessons from Practice', in P. Evans, Y. Doz and A. Laurent (eds) *Human Resource Management in International Firms*, London: Macmillan.

Evans, R. (1990) 'The Last Frontier', *International Management*, April:16–20.

Eyraud, F., Marsden, D. and Silvestre, J-J. (1990) 'Occupational and internal labour markets in Britain and France', *International Labour Review* 129(4):501–17.

Fairburn, J.A. and Kay, J.A. (eds) (1989) *Mergers and Merger Policy*, Oxford: Oxford University Press.

Farr, M. (1989) 'The New Arms Merchants', *International Management* December:28–30.

Ford, D. (ed.) (1990) *Understanding Business Markets: Interaction, Relationships, Networks*, London: Academic Press.

Forster, N. (1991) 'Employee Job Mobility and Relocation: A Major Challenge for Human Resource Managers in the 1990s', *Personnel Review* 19(6):18–24.

Forster, N. (1992) 'International managers and mobile families: the professional and personal dynamics of trans-national career pathing and job mobility in the 1990s', *International Journal of Human Resource Management* 3(3):605–23.

Froebel, F., Heinrichs, J. and Kreye, O. (1980) *The New International Division of Labour*, Cambridge: Cambridge University Press.

Gallo, M.A. (1988) 'The Role of the General Manager in the First Stages of Internationalization', Instituto de Estudios Superiores de la Empresa, Universidad de Navarra.

Gallo, M.A. and Luostarinen, R. (1991) 'Internationalization: A Challenging Change for Family Business', Instituto de Estudios Superiores de la Empresa, Universidad de Navarra.

Gallo, M.A. and Sveen, J. (1991) 'Internationalizing the Family Business: Facilitating and Restraining Factors', *Family Business Review* iv(2):181–90.

Geringer, J.M., Beamish, P.W. and daCosta, R. (1989) 'Diversification Strategy and Internationalization: Implications for MNE Performance', *Strategic Management Journal* 10:109–19.

Geroski, P. (1988) 'Competition and innovation', in *Research on the "Costs of Non-Europe"*, vol. 2, Luxembourg: Commission of the European Communities.

Gertsen, M.C. (1990) 'Intercultural competence and expatriates', *International Journal of Human Resource Management* 1(3):341–62.

Ghoshal, S. (1987) 'Global Strategy: An Organising Framework', *Strategic Management Journal* 8:425–40.

Gill, J. (1988) *Factors Affecting the Survival and Growth of the Smaller Company*, Aldershot: Gower.

Goold, M. and Campbell, A. (1987) *Strategies and Styles: The Role of the Centre in Managing Diversified Organizations*, Oxford: Blackwell.

Grant, R.M. (1991) 'The Resource-Based Theory of Competitive Advantage: Implications for Strategy Formation', *California Management Review* 33(3):114–35.

Grootings, P. (1989) 'A European directory of occupational profiles', *Vocational Training* 3:21–4.

Grosser, A. (1989) 'The future of education in Europe', *Vocational Training* 1:28–30.

Hakansson, H. and Johanson, J. (1988) 'Formal and Informal Cooperation Strategies in International Industrial Networks', in F.J. Contractor and P. Lorange (eds) *Cooperative Strategies in International Business*, Lexington Mass.: Lexington Books.

Hall, M. (1990) 'UK employment practices after the social charter', *Personnel Management* March:32–5.

Hallen, L. and Wiedersheim-Paul, F. (1979) 'Psychic distance and buyer–seller interaction', *Organisation, Markand och Samhalle* 16(5):308–24.

Hamel, G. (1991) 'Competition for Competence and Inter-Partner Learning within International Strategic Alliances', *Strategic Management Journal* 12:83–103.

Hamel, G. and Prahalad, P.K. (1989) 'Strategic intent', *Harvard Business Review*, May–June:63–76.

Hampden-Turner, C. (1990) *Corporate Culture for Competitive Edge: A User's Guide*, Special Report No. 1195, London: Economist Publications.

Handy, C. (1987) *The Making of Managers: a Report on Management Education in the United States, West Germany, France, Japan, and the UK*, London: NEDO/MSC.

Harper, S.C. (1988) 'Now that the Dust has Settled: Learning from Japanese Management', *Business Horizons* July–August.

Harrigan, K.R. (1986) *Managing for Joint Venture Success*, Lexington, Mass.: Lexington Books.

—— (1988) 'Joint ventures and competitive strategy', *Strategic Management Journal* 9:141–58.

Harris, P.R. and Harris, D.L. (1972) 'Training for cultural understanding', *Training and Development Journal*: 8–10.

Harrison, R. and Hopkins, R.L. (1967) 'The design of cross-cultural training: an alternative to the university model', *Journal of Applied Behavioural Science* 3(4):431–60.

Hawes, F. and Kealey, D.J. (1981) 'Canadians in Development: An

Empirical Study of Canadian Technical Assistance', *International Journal of Intercultural Relations* 5:239–58.

Hayes, R.H. and Wheelwright, S.C. (1984) *Restoring our Competitive Edge: Competing through Manufacturing*, New York: Wiley.

Hayes, C., Anderson, A. and Fonda, N. (1984) *Competence and Competition: Training and Education in the Federal Republic of Germany, the United States, and Japan*, London: NEDO/MSC.

Hedlund, G. and Kverneland, A. (1985) 'Are Strategies for Foreign Market Entry Changing? The Case of Swedish Investment in Japan', *International Studies of Management and Organisation* 15:41–59.

Hegewisch, A. (1992) 'Equal Opportunities Policies and Developments in Human Resource Management: A Comparative European Analysis', Cranfield School of Management.

Heller, F.A. and Yukl, G. (1969) 'Participation, Managerial Decision-Making and Situational Variables', *Organisational Behaviour and Human Performance* 4:227–41.

Hendry, C. (1990) 'The Corporate Management of Human Resources under Conditions of Decentralization', *British Journal of Management* 1(2):91–103.

Hendry, C. (1991) 'International comparisons of human resource management: putting the firm in the frame', *International Journal of Human Resource Management* 2(3):415–40.

Hendry, C. (1994) *Human Resource Management: A Strategic Approach to Employment*, London: Butterworth-Heinemann.

Hendry, C. and Pettigrew, A. (1987) 'Banking on HRM to Respond to Change', *Personnel Management* November:29–32.

—— (1989) 'Strategic Change and Human Resource Management in Pilkington plc', Centre for Corporate Strategy and Change, University of Warwick.

—— (1990) 'Human resource management: an agenda for the 1990s', *International Journal of Human Resource Management* 1(1):17–43.

—— (1992) *The Processes of Internationalization and the Implications for Human Resource Management and Human Resource Development*, Sheffield: Department of Employment.

Hendry, C., Arthur, M.B. and Jones, A.M. (1991) 'Learning from Doing: Adaptation and Resource Management in the Smaller Firm', paper given to the 11th Annual Strategic Management Society Conference, Toronto, October.

—— (work in progress) *Strategy through People: Human Resource Activity in the Smaller Enterprise*.

Hendry, C., Jones, A.M. and Arthur, M.B. (1991) 'Skill Supply, Training, and Development in the Small–Medium Enterprise', *International Small Business Journal* 10(1):68–72.

Hendry, C., Jones, A.M., Arthur, M.B. and Pettigrew, A. (1991) *Human Resource Development in the Small–Medium Enterprise*, Sheffield: Department of Employment.

Hickson, K., McMillan, C.J., Azumi, K. and Horvath, D. (1979) 'Grounds for Comparative Organization Theory: Quicksands or Hardcore?', in

C.J. Lammars and D.J. Hickson (eds) *Organizations Alike and Unlike*, London: Routledge and Kegan Paul.

The Higher (1991a) 'Britain's brightest flock to Europe', August, 16:2.

—— (1991b) 'Erasmus hampered by cash shortage', October:4.

—— (1991c) 'Languages for all in 1992 countdown', October:11.

Hofstede, G. (1980) *Culture's Consequences*, California: Sage.

—— (1991) *Cultures and Organizations: Software of the Mind. Intercultural Cooperation and its Importance for Survival*, Maidenhead: McGraw-Hill.

Holden, L. (1991) 'European trends in training and development', *International Journal of Human Resource Management* 2(2):113–31.

Horvath, D., McMillan, C.J., Azumi, K. and Hickson, K. (1976) 'The Cultural Context of Organizational Control', *International Studies of Management and Organization* 6:60–86.

Husen, T. (1989) 'Integration of general and vocational education – An international perspective', *Vocational Training* 1:9–13.

Hyman, R. and Ferner, A. (eds) (1992) *Industrial Relations in the New Europe*, Oxford: Blackwell.

Hymer, S.M. (1976) 'The international operations of national firms', Cambridge, Mass.: MIT Press.

IDS/IPM (1988) *1992: Personnel Management and the Single European Market*, London: Income Data Services/Institute of Personnel Management.

Inkpen, A.C. (1991) 'Japanese–North American Joint Venture Strategies and Organisational Learning', paper given to to the 11th Annual Strategic Management Society Conference, Toronto, October.

Institute for Employment Research (1991) 'Employment in the Single European Market', Bulletin No. 10, University of Warwick.

Institute of Manpower Studies (1987) 'Relocating Managers and Professional Staff', IMS Report No. 139, Sussex University.

—— (1989) *How Many Graduates in the Twenty-First Century*, IMS, University of Sussex.

International Management (1986) 'Expansion abroad: the new direction for European firms', November.

Itami, H. with T.W. Roehl (1987) *Mobilizing Invisible Assets*, Cambridge, Mass.: Harvard University Press.

Jakobsen, L. and Martinussen, J. (1991) 'A national incentive scheme for establishing cooperation between small firms', paper given to the ICSB 36th Annual Conference, Vienna, June.

Jarillo, J.C. (1988) 'On Strategic Networks', *Strategic Management Journal* 9:31–41.

Jarillo, J.-C. and Martinez, J.I. (1990) 'Competition and Cooperation in International Strategy', Lausanne: IMD.

Jelinek, M. and Adler, N.J. (1988) 'Women: World-Class Managers for Global Competition', *Academy of Management Executive* 2(1):11–19.

Johanson, J. and Mattsson, L-G. (1988) 'Internationalization in Industrial Systems – A Network Approach', in N. Hood and J-E. Vahlne (eds) *Strategies in Global Competition*, London: Croom Helm.

Johanson, J. and Vahlne J-E. (1977) 'The Internationalization Process of the Firm – A Model of Knowledge Development and Increasing Foreign Commitment', *Journal of International Business Studies* 8(1):23–32.

—— (1990) 'The Mechanism of Internationalization', *International Marketing Review* 7(4):11–24.

—— (1991) 'The management of internationalisation', Warwick/Venice Workshop on 'Perspectives on Strategic Change: Studying Organisations and Environments as Processes', Venice, May.

Johanson, J. and Wiedersheim-Paul, F. (1975) 'The Internationalization of the Firm – Four Swedish Cases', *Journal of Management Studies* 12:305–22.

Johnson, G. (1987) *Strategic Change and the Management Process*, Oxford: Basil Blackwell.

Johnston, J. (1991) 'An Empirical Study of the Repatriation of Managers in UK Multinationals', *Human Resource Management Journal* 1(4):102–9.

Kaikati, J. (1989) 'Europe 1992 – Mind your Strategic P's and Q's', *Sloan Management Review* Fall:85–92.

Kanter, R.M. (1989) *When Giants Learn to Dance*, New York: Simon & Schuster.

Kay, N.M. (1990) 'Competition, Technological Change and 1992', Department of Economics, University of Strathclyde.

Keenan, T. (1991) 'Graduate Recruitment à la Française', *Personnel Management* December:34–7.

Keep, E. (1992) 'Big British Companies – No Longer What They Seem', VET Forum Conference, University of Warwick, June.

Kerr, C., Dunlop, J.T., Harbin, F.H., and Myers, C.A. (1960) *Industrialism and Industrial Man*, London: Heinemann.

Killing, J.P. (1983) *Strategies for Joint Venture Success*, New York: Praeger.

Kitching, J. (1967) 'Why do Mergers Miscarry?', *Harvard Business Review* November–December:84–101.

Kobrin, S.J. (1988) 'Expatriate Reduction and Strategic Control in American Multinationals', *Human Resource Management* 27(1):63–75.

Korn/Ferry International (1986) *A Survey of Corporation Leaders in the '80s*, New York: Korn/Ferry International.

Krulis-Randa, J.S. (1990) 'Strategic human resource management (SHRM) in Europe after 1992', *International Journal of Human Resource Management* 1(2):131–9.

Labour Research Department (1989) *Europe 1992: What It All Means to Trade Unionists*, London: LRD.

Landis, D. and Brislin, R. (1983) *Handbook on Intercultural Training*, Vol. 1, New York: Pergamon Press.

Lansberg, I., Perrow, E.L. and Rogolsky, S. (1988) 'Family business as an emerging field', *Family Business Review* 1(1):1–7.

Lane, C. (1990) 'Vocational Training and New Production Concepts in Germany: Some Lessons for Britain', *Industrial Relations Journal* 21(4):247–59.

—— (1991) 'Industrial reorganisation in Europe: patterns of convergence and divergence in Germany, France and Britain', *Work, Employment and Society* 5(4):515–39.

Laurent, A. (1986) 'The Cross-Cultural Puzzle of International Human Resource Management', *Human Resource Management* 25(1):91–102.

Lawrence, P.A. (1980) *Managers and Management in West Germany*, London: Croom Helm.
—— (1991) 'The personnel function: An Anglo-German comparison', in C. Brewster and S. Tyson (eds) *International Comparisons in Human Resource Management*, London: Pitman.
Lester, T. (1991) 'A structure for Europe', *Management Today* January:76–8.
Levitt, T. (1983) 'The globalization of markets', *Harvard Business Review* May–June:92–102.
Lincoln, J.R., Hanada, M. and Olsen, J. (1981) 'Cultural Orientations and Individual Reactions to Organisations', *Administrative Science Quarterly* 26:93–115.
Lindell, M. and Melin, L. (1991) 'Diversified Renewal through Strategic Bridging – Acquisition and Realization of Visions', paper given to the 11th Annual International Conference of the Strategic Management Society, Toronto, October.
Lloyd, T., Carton-Kelly, A., and Mueller, M. (1991) 'EC Heavyweights', *International Management* April:26–67.
Lobel, S.A. (1990) 'Global Leadership Competencies: Managing to a Different Drumbeat', *Human Resource Management* 29(1):39–47.
Locke, R. (1991) 'Mastering the Lingo', *The Higher* 5 April:23–5.
Lorange, P. (1986) 'Human Resource Management in Multinational Cooperative Ventures', *Human Resource Management* 25(1):133–48.
Lubatkin, M. (1983) 'Mergers and the Performance of the Acquiring Firm', *Acadamy of Management Review* 8(2):218–25.
Luostarinen, R. (1979) *Internationalization of the Firm*, Helsinki: Helsinki School of Economics.
Lyons, M.P. (1991) 'Joint Ventures as Strategic Choice – A Literature Review', *Long Range Planning* 24(4):130–44.
MacDonald, S., Pettigrew, A., Gustavsson, P. and Melin, L. (1991) 'The Learning Process Behind the European Activities of Large UK and Swedish Firms', EIBA 17th Annual Conference, Copenhagen, December.
McKiernan, P. (1992) *Strategies of Growth*, London: Routledge.
Mangham, I.L. (1978) *Interactions, Organisations and Interventions: A Dramaturgical Perspective on Organisation Development*, London: Wiley.
Marginson, P. (1992) 'Multinational Britain: Employment and work in an International Economy', VET Forum Conference on 'Multinational Companies and Human Resources: A Moveable Feast?', University of Warwick, June.
Martin, S. and Hartley, K. (1991) 'European Collaboration in Aerospace: Recent Trends and Future Prospects', *European Research* 2(6):14–19.
Mendenhall, M. and Oddou, G. (1985) 'The Dimensions of Expatriate Acculturation: A Review', *Academy of Management Review* 10:39–47.
Mendenhall, M., Dunbar, E. and Oddou, G. (1987) 'Expatriate Selection, Training, and Career Pathing: A Review and Critique', *Human Resource Management* 26:331–45.
Millington, A.I. and Bayliss, B.T. (1990) 'The Process of Internationalisation: UK Companies in the EC', *Management International Review* 30(2):151–61.

Mintzberg, H. (1973) *The Nature of Managerial Work*, New York: Harper & Row.

Moran, Stahl and Boyer (1989) 'A report on expatriation and repatriation of Fortune 500 client firms', paper given to the Academy of Management Annual Conference, New Orleans, August.

Morris, D. and Hergert, M. (1987) 'Trends in international collaborative agreements', *Columbia Journal of World Business* XXII(2):15–21.

Mosley, H.G. (1990) 'The social dimension of European integration', *International Labour Review* 129(2):147–64.

Murray, F.T. and Murray, A.H. (1985) 'SMR forum: Global managers for global businesses', *Sloan Management Review* Winter.

Neale, R. and Mindel, R. (1992) 'Rigging up Multicultural Teamworking', *Personnel Management* January:36–9.

Negandhi, A. (1979) 'Convergence in Organisational Practices: An Empirical Study of Industrial Enterprises in Developing Countries', in C.J. Lammers and D.J. Hickson (eds) *Organisations Alike and Unlike*, London: Routledge and Kegan Paul.

Nielsen, N.C. (1989) 'Network Cooperation – Achieving Competitiveness in a Global Economy', Taastrup: Danish Technological Institute.

OECD (1989) 'Employment outlook', July.

Ohmae, K. (1985) *Triad Power: The Coming Shape of Global Competition*, New York: Free Press.

Ondrack, D. (1985) 'International Human Resources Management in European and North American Firms', *International Studies of Management and Organisation* 15(1):6–32.

Oulton, N. (1990) 'Quality and performance in UK trade, 1978–87', NIESR Discussion Paper No. 197, National Institute of Economic and Social Research, London.

Parry, J. (1990) 'Telecommunications: special survey', *International Management* October:55–68.

Pavitt, K. and Patel, P. (1990) 'Large Firms and the Production of the World's Technology: A Case of Non-Globalisation', Science Policy Research Unit, Sussex University.

Peat Marwick McLintock (1991) 'UK Business Expansion Falls Behind Other Major EC Countries', 3 June.

Perlmutter, H.V. (1969) 'The Tortuous Evolution of the Multinational Corporation', *Columbia Journal of World Business* Jan–Feb:9–18.

Pescotto, G. (1992) 'EC Banking in the 1990s: Cooperation or Competition?' *European Research* 3(1):1–6.

Pettigrew, A., Hendry, C., and Sparrow, P. (1989) *Training in Britain: Employers' Perspectives on Human Resources*, London: HMSO.

Pieper, R. (ed.) (1990) *Human Resource Management: An International Comparison*, Berlin: Walter de Gruyter.

Pietsch, M. (1991) 'Is Transnational Cooperation a Strategic Option for SMEs in 1993?', paper given to 14th National Small Firms Policy and Research Conference, Blackpool, November.

Piore, M.J. and Sabel, C.F. (1984) *The Second Industrial Divide*, New York: Basic Books.

Porter, M.E. (1980) *Competitive Strategy*, New York: Free Press.

—— *Competitive Advantage*, New York: Free Press.

—— (1986) 'Changing Patterns of International Competition', *California Management Review* 28(2):9–40.

—— (1990) *The Competitive Advantage of Nations*, London: Macmillan.

Prahalad, C.K. (1987) *The multinational mission*, New York: Free Press.

Prahalad, C.K. (1990) 'Globalisation: The Intellectual and Managerial Challenges', *Human Resource Management* 29(1):27–37.

Prais, S.J. and Wagner, K. (1988) 'Productivity and Management: The Training of Foremen in Britain and Germany', *National Institute Economic Review*, No. 123.

Price Waterhouse/Cranfield (1990) *The Price Waterhouse/Cranfield Project on International Strategic Human Resource Management: Report 1990*, London: Price Waterhouse.

Pucik, V. (1988) 'Strategic alliances, organisational learning and competitive advantage', *Human Resource Management* 27(1):77–93.

Rainbird, H. (1992) 'The European Dimension of Training', in M. Gold (ed.) *Europe: the Social Dimension*, London: Macmillan.

Rajan, A. (1990) *1992: A Zero-Sum Game*, London: Industrial Society Press.

Ramsay, H. (1990) '1992 – The Year of the Multinational? Corporate Behaviour, Industrial Restructuring and Labour in the Single Market', *Warwick Papers in Industrial Relations No. 35* IRRU, University of Warwick, November.

—— (1991) 'The Community, the Multinational, its Workers and their Charter: A Modern Tale of Industrial Democracy', *Work, Employment and Society* 5(4):541–66.

Randlesome, C., Brierley, W., Bruton, K., Gordon, C. and King, P. (1990) *Business Cultures in Europe*, Oxford: Heinemann.

Ratiu, I. (1983) 'Thinking internationally: A comparison of how international executives learn', *International Studies of Management and Organisation* 13(1–2):139–50.

Reich, R.B. and Mankin, E.D. (1986) 'Joint ventures with Japan give away our future', *Harvard Business Review* March-April:78–86.

Reilly, R.R. and Campbell, B. (1990) 'How Corporate Performance Measurement Systems Inhibit Globalisation', *Human Resource Management* 29(1):63–8.

Retuerto, E. (1989) 'Information on qualifications: An important variable for vocational training at Community level', *Vocational Training* 3:2–4.

Reynolds, C. (1986) 'Compensation of Overseas Personnel', in J.J. Famularo (ed.) *Handbook of Human Resources Administration*, 2nd edn, New York: McGraw-Hill.

Rogot, J. (1990) 'Human Resource Management in France', in R. Pieper (ed.) *Human Resource Management: An International Comparison*, Berlin: Walter de Gruyter.

Ronen, S. (1989) 'Training the International Assignee', in I. Goldstein (ed.) *Training and Career Development*, San Francisco: Jossey-Bass.

Root, F. (1988) 'Some taxonomies of international cooperative agreements', in F. Contractor and P. Lorange (eds) *Cooperative Strategies in International Business*, Lexington, Mass.: Lexington Books.

Root, F.R. (1986) 'Staffing the Overseas Unit', in J.J. Formularo (ed.) *Handbook of Human Resources Administration*, 2nd edn, New York: McGraw-Hill.

Rosenfeld, R., Whipp, R. and Pettigrew, A. (1989) 'Processes of internationalization: Regeneration and Competitiveness', *Economia Aziendale* VIII,(1):21–47.

Rothwell, S. (1992) 'The Development of the International Manager', *Personnel Management* January:33–5.

Ruben, D. and Kealey, D.J. (1983) 'Personnel Selection', in D. Landis and R. Brislin (eds) *Handbook on Intercultural Training*, Vol. 1, New York: Pergamon Press.

Rugman, A.M. (1981) *Inside the Multinationals*, London: Croom Helm.

—— (1986) 'New theories of the multinational enterprise: an assessment of internalisation theory', *Bulletin of Economic Research* 38(2):101–18.

Rumelt, R.P. (1974) *Strategy, Structure and Economic Performance*, Cambridge, Mass.: Harvard University Press.

Salt, J. and Kitching, R. (1990) 'Foreign workers and the UK labour market', *Employment Gazette* November:538–46.

Salter, M.S. (1973) 'Stages of Corporate Development', in B. Taylor and K. MacMillan (eds) *Business Policy*, Bradford: Crosby Lockford.

Sasseen, J. (1989) 'Car-Nage', *International Management* December:20–7.

Schillaci, C.E. (1987) 'Designing successful joint ventures', *Journal of Business Strategy* 8(2):59–63.

Schneider, S.C. (1988) 'National vs. Corporate Culture: Implications for Human Resource Management', *Human Resource Management* 27(2):231–46.

Schuler, R.S. and Dowling, P.J. (1988) 'Survey of ASPA/1 Members', Stern School of Business, New York University.

Schuler, R.S., Dowling, P.J., and De Cieri, H. (1993) 'An Integrative Framework of Strategic Human Resource Management', *International Journal of Human Resource Management* (forthcoming).

Schwind, H. (1985) 'The State of the Art in Cross-Cultural Management Training', in R. Doktor (ed.) *International Human Resource Development Annual*, Vol. 1.

Scott, B.R. (1971) *Strategies of Corporate Development*, Cambridge, Mass.: Harvard Business School.

Scullion, H. (1991) 'Why Companies Prefer to Use Expatriates', *Personnel Management* November:32–5.

—— (1992) 'Attracting management globetrotters', *Personnel Management* January:28–32.

Sellin, B. (1989) 'The recognition and/or comparability of non-university vocational training qualifications in the Member States of the European Communities', *Vocational Training* 3:5–10.

Sisson, K., Waddington, J. and Whitston, C. (1992) 'The Structure of Capital in the European Community: The Size of Companies and the Implications for Industrial Relations', Warwick Papers in Industrial Relations, No. 38, University of Warwick.

Smith, C. (1990) 'How are Engineers Formed? Professionals, Nation and Class', *Work, Employment and Society* 4(3):451–70.

Spivey, W.A. and Thomas, L.D. (1990) 'Global Management: Concepts, Themes, Problems, and Research issues', *Human Resource Management* 29(1):85–97.

Stanworth, J. and Gray, C. (eds) (1991) *Bolton 20 years On: The Small Firm in the 1990s*, London: Paul Chapman.

Stopford, J.M. and Turner, L. (1985) *Britain and the Multinationals*, Chichester: Wiley.

—— and Wells, L.T. Jr. (1972) *Managing the Multinational Enterprise*, New York: Basic Books.

Sullivan, D. and Bauerschmidt, A. (1990) 'Incremental Internationalization: A Test of Johanson and Vahlne's Thesis', *Management International Review* 30(1):19–30.

Szarka, J. (1990) 'Networking and small firms', *International Small Business Journal* 8(2):10–22.

Takahashi, Y. (1990) 'Human Resource Management in Japan', in R. Pieper (ed.) *Human Resource Management: An International Comparison*, Berlin: Walter de Gruyter.

Teece, D.J. (ed.) (1987) *The Competitive Challenge: Strategies for Industrial Innovation and Renewal*, Cambridge, Mass.: Ballinger.

Teece, D.J. (1987) 'Profiting from technological innovation: Implications for integration, collaboration, licensing, and public policy', in D.J. Teece (ed.) *The Competitive Challenge: Strategies for Industrial Innovation and Renewal*, Cambridge, Mass.: Ballinger.

Thorelli, H.B. (1986) 'Networks: between markets and hierarchies', *Strategic Management Journal* 7:37–51.

Thurley, K. (1990) 'Towards a European Approach to Personnel Management', *Personnel Management* September:54–7.

—— (1991) 'The utilisation of human resources: A proposed approach', in C. Brewster and S. Tyson (eds) *International Comparisons in Human Resource Management*, London: Pitman.

Tigner, B. (1990) 'Half-Way to the Euro Company', *International Management* May:46–50.

Torbiorn, I. (1982) *Living Abroad: Personal Adjustment and Personnel Policy in the Overseas Setting*, New York: Wiley.

Trepo, G. (1975) 'Mise en place d'une D.P.O.: Le rôle crucial de la direction', *Direction et Gestion* 1.

Tully, S. (1988) 'Europe's Best Business Schools', *Fortune* 117(11):106–10.

Tung, R.L. (1982) 'Selection and Training Procedures of US, European and Japanese Multinationals', *California Management Review* 25(1):57–71.

—— (1988) 'Career issues in international assignments', *Academy of Management Executive* 11(3):241–48.

—— (1989) 'International Assignments: Strategic Challenges in the 21st Century', paper given to Academy of Management International Management Symposium on 'Career Issues', Washington, DC, August.

Tybejee, T.T. (1988) 'Japan's joint ventures in the United States', in F.J. Contractor and P. Lorange (eds) *Cooperative Strategies in International Business*, Lexington, Mass.: Lexington Books.

United Nations Centre on Transnational Corporations (1988) *Trans-*

national Corporations in World Development: Trends and Prospects, New York: UN.

Vernon, R. (1966) 'International Investment and International Trade in the Product Cycle', *Quarterly Journal of Economics* 80, May:190–207.

—— (1971) *Sovereignty at Bay*, New York: Basic Books.

—— (1977) *Storm over the multinationals*, Cambridge, MA: Harvard University Press.

—— (1979) 'The product cycle hypothesis in a new international environment', *Oxford Bulletin of Economics and Statistics* 41:255–68.

Wachter, H. and Stengelhofen, T. (1992) 'Human Resource Management in a Unified Germany', *Employee Relations* 14(2):21–37.

Wagner, K. (1991) 'Training Efforts and Industrial Efficiency in West Germany', in J. Stevens and R. Mackay (eds) *Training and Competitiveness*, London: NEDO/Kogan Page.

Warner, M. (1987) 'Industrialization, Management Education and Training Systems: A Comparative Analysis', *Journal of Management Studies* 24(1):91–112.

—— (1991) 'How Japanese Managers Learn', paper given to Warwick Business School, International Business Seminar Series, June.

Webster, F.E., Jr. (1979) *Industrial Marketing Strategy*, New York: Wiley.

Weick, K.E. and Van Orden, P.W. (1990) 'Organising on a Global Scale: A Research and Teaching Agenda', *Human Resource Management* 29(1):49–61.

Welch, L.S. (1985) 'The International Marketing of Technology: An Interaction Perspective', *International Marketing Review* 2(1):41–53.

Welch, L.S. and Luostarinen, R. (1988) 'Internationalization: Evolution of a Concept', *Journal of General Management* 14(2).

Welch, L.S. and Wiedersheim-Paul, F. (1980) 'Initial exports: a marketing failure query', *Journal of Management Studies* October:333–44.

Welsch, J. (1991) 'Family Enterprises in the United Kingdom, the Federal Republic of Germany, and Spain: A Transnational Comparison', *Family Business Review* iv(2):191–203.

Whipp, R. (1991) 'Human resource management, strategic change and competition: the role of learning', *International Journal of Human Resource Management* 2(2):165–92.

Williams, K., Williams, J. and Haslam, C. (1989) 'Why take the stocks out? Britain versus Japan', *International Journal of Operations and Production Management* 9(8).

Williamson, O.E. (1975) *Markets and Hierarchies: Analysis and Antitrust Implications: a Study of the Economics of Internal Organizations*, New York: Free Press.

Williamson, P.J. (1990) 'Winning the Export War: British, Japanese and West German Exporters' Strategy Compared', *British Journal of Management* 1(4):215–30.

Windolf, P. (1986) 'Recruitment, Selection, and Internal Labour Markets in Britain and Germany', *Organisation Studies* 7(3):235–54.

Wood, S. and Peccei, R. (1990) 'Preparing for 1992? Business-Led Versus Strategic Human Resource Management', *Human Resource Management Journal* 1(1):63–89.

Yamin, M. and Batstone, S.J. (1987) 'Determinants of Multinational Entry via Acquisition of Domestic Firms: An Inter-Industry Analysis', Department of Economics, Trent Polytechnic.

Yip, G. (1989) 'Global strategy . . . in a world of nations?' *Sloan Management Review* 31(1):20–41.

Young, S., Hamill, J., Wheeler, C. and Davies, J.R. (1989) *International Market Entry and Development: Strategies and Management,* Hemel Hempstead: Harvester Wheatsheaf.

Index